£2.25

Look in POP ANNUAL

POP FEATURES!

CONTENTS

Published by ITV Books Ltd 247 Tottenham Court Road London W1P 0AU

Editor: Neil Tennant Designer: Richard Krzyzak Cover design: Hamish
Production: Aardvark Books Ltd Made and printed in Great Britain
ISBN 0 907965 05 9

For many months now the pop charts have been buzzing with synthesizers and thumping to computerised drums. Is this some kind of electronic revolution? Hang on to your Human League records as* Dave Rimmer *tells you all you need to know (well, almost) about...

ElecTro

Pop

IN THE BEGINNING

These days, a synthesizer can be small enough to fit into a briefcase. Fans at early Depeche Mode concerts were often surprised to find the band going home on the same train as themselves – and with their equipment too! But when the first synthesizer was built by RCA in 1954 it was so big that it filled a room. It wasn't until 1964 that, with the aid of transistors, American electronics engineer Dr Robert Moog developed one small and portable enough to be of much use to musicians.

At the time, people imagined Moog's synthesizer to be some kind of robot that played itself and criticized it for being 'non-musical'. Moog pointed out that it was an instrument like any other, and was no less natural than 'a box with holes in it in the shape of an "f", with maple on one side and spruce on the other...'

Soon, the electronic sounds of the synthesizer began to appear on records. The Monkees' LP, *Pisces, Capricorn, Aquarius and Jones*, in 1967 was the first to use it. But the synthesizer wasn't really recognized as an instrument until 1968, when a gent by the name of Walter Carlos made what was to become the biggest-selling classical record of all time. Called *Switched-On Bach*, it was a selection of some of Bach's best known pieces played entirely on

Kraftwerk (*left and below*)

one of Moog's synthesizers. Many people since have tried to imitate Carlos' success. Only Japanese synthesist Tomita – who also plays electronic versions of popular classics – has come close.

ALTER AND DISTORT

In Britain in the early 1970s, classically-trained musicians like ELP's Keith Emerson – who used to attack his Hammond organ with a knife to try and liven up his concerts – and Rick Wakeman of Yes began using the synthesizer to show off their skills at playing. The problem was, they just played it the same way as they did their organs and pianos.

Roxy Music, whose debut album appeared in 1972, was the first British group to use synthesizers in an original way. Apart from adding bleeps and whistles to most of their tracks and a surprisingly catchy synthesizer passage to their first hit single "Virginia Plain", Roxy's electronics wizard Brian Eno also used electronics to alter and distort the sounds of the other instruments in the group.

Apparently because of arguments with their singer Bryan Ferry about who was the star of the show, Eno left Roxy Music after their second album. He went on to become a very influential figure indeed – making his own experimental solo albums as well as working with the likes of David Bowie, Ultravox and Talking Heads. Eno was perhaps the first true "synthesist", as opposed to a keyboard player using a synthesizer.

Meanwhile in Germany, different things were happening. Classical composer Karl-Heinz Stockhausen had been using electronics for years. In the early 1970s young musicians, many of them former students of Stockhausen, began turning to the synthesizer in a big way. They were helped by the fact that, unlike Britain and

America which both had a history of rock and roll music, there was no-one to frown at a group which didn't use the standard guitars/bass/keyboards/drums line-up.

Kraftwerk were probably the most interesting and influential group to emerge at that time, but there were also experimental groups like Can, Amon Duul, Faust and Tangerine Dream. Though many people just regarded their music as a horrible noise (often it was!), Germany became known as the place where the possibilities of electronic music were being explored. It's worth noting that Bowie and Eno chose Germany to record their first two collaborations – *Low* and *Heroes*. They were made at the Cologne studio of electronic producer Conny Plank, as were Ultravox's *Vienna* and *Rage in Eden* albums.

Kraftwerk's "Autobahn" – a joky piece based on the sounds of the motorway – had been a massive American disco hit in 1975. In 1977, Munich producer Giorgio Moroder harnessed the synthesizer to his own brand of disco music. The result was an international hit with Donna Summer's "I Feel Love". What marked that record off from others was an electronic beat made with a "sequencer" – a device which repeats as often and as quickly as you like any series of notes which is fed into it. The sequencer beat soon became standard fare on many disco records.

THE MUSIC TRAVELS

By the late '70s, with synthesizers becoming ever cheaper and more portable, electronic groups began springing up everywhere. In Japan, the Yellow Magic Orchestra began shaping up like a Far Eastern version of Kraftwerk. A Belgian group called Telex made an unforgettable electronic version of the original rock 'n' roll song: "Rock Around the Clock".

A whole clutch of bands appeared in Britain. The Human League and Ultravox were among the first, but they got overlooked in the days of punk and had to wait a few years before finding chart success. Orchestral Manoeuvres in the Dark arrived around then too, with a debut single "Electricity" that some thought sounded suspiciously like Kraftwerk.

Many of the groups at that time like Cabaret Voltaire and Throbbing Gristle made dull and gloomy music which earnt them the label "industrial". A lot of people began thinking of electronic music as grey, serious and no fun at all.

It was a stern-looking young man called Gary Numan who began to shake off that image when, in 1979, he scored a number one hit with "Are Friends Electric", and then again with "Cars". From then on, Numan's hits came one after another. People who had sneered at the synthesizer began to realize that it could be fun after all.

THE FUTURISTS

In 1980, a new movement began to flourish in London's clubs. Called the "New Romantics" at first, and then "Futurists", they grew up on a diet of Kraftwerk, Bowie and Eno, and soon began making their own electronic music. Along with Midge Ure and Billy Currie from Ultravox, club host and DJ Steve Strange and Rusty Egan formed Visage. Another group of clubgoers bought synthesizers and called themselves Spandau Ballet, though later they traded their electronics for funk.

As people began to realize that electronics wasn't just something that came up in physics lessons, more and more synthesizer groups appeared. Depeche Mode arrived from Basildon in Essex. Soft Cell turned up from Leeds. Birmingham brought us Duran Duran. A London group called Japan who'd been playing with synthesizers for years without anybody noticing suddenly came into fashion. Ultravox rocketed to the top of the charts with "Vienna". In early 1982, even the granddaddies of it all – Kraftwerk – made a welcome return to the British charts.

Gary Numan once said: 'To be honest, I'm not that good a player at all. I can get quite nice sounds. I know what all the dials do on a Minimoog. I know what the gadgets are and I can use them quite well.'

And with a little bit of practice – instead of the years it can take to learn the guitar – so can anybody. Synthesizers have never been cheaper and easier to use than they are today. Electronic music, it seems, is here to stay.

DEPECHE MODE

'I don't think the people who come to see us now think of us as a

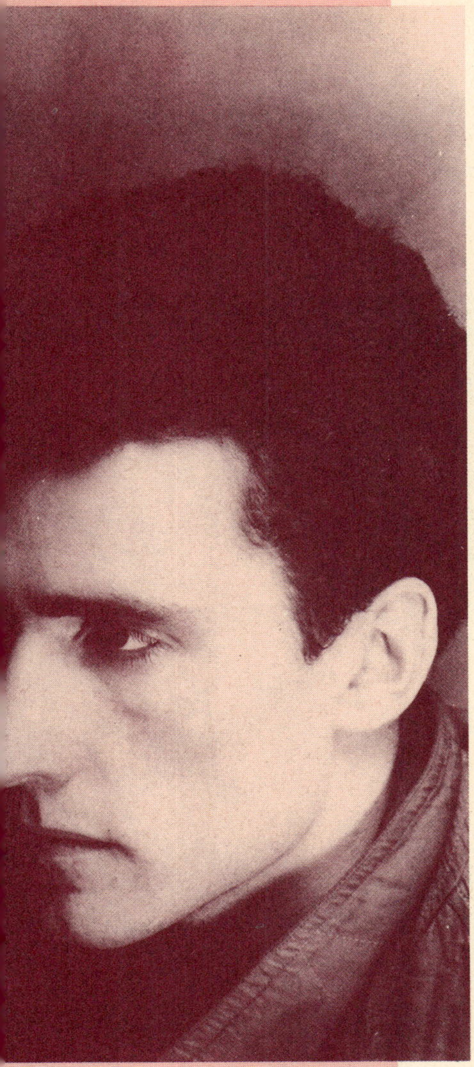

synthesizer band,' says Depeche Mode singer Dave Gahan. 'We're just a band playing music, and we use synthesizers exactly the same way a guitar band uses guitars, with bass, rhythm and lead parts. Of course we also have drums on tape but basically the synthesizer is just another instrument.'

Hang on. Didn't Dr Robert Moog say something like that 18 years ago? Dave's probably also put his finger on why synthesized music has lost the "gloom and doom" tag: it's not the instruments you use, but what you play with them. For these boys from Basildon, that means light, bright electro-pop.

Formed in 1980, and originally a two guitar/one synth band, Depeche Mode's first gig was at an under-12s' disco in Basildon. A series of concerts at a club called Crocs in nearby Rayleigh followed, but it was while playing at a "futurist night" at the Bridge House in London's Canning Town that they were seen by Daniel Miller of Mute Records.

They had a track on *Some Bizarre*, a 1981 compilation of new electronic groups, and then a first single on Mute, "Dreaming of Me", which made the lower end of the charts. But after that, they had no trouble making the top ten with catchy songs like "New Life", "I Just Can't Get Enough" and "See You".

For now, their only problem with synthesizers is knowing exactly what to *do* on stage... but they're working on it.

ORCHESTRAL MANOEUVRES IN THE DARK

'I think,' Andy McCluskey of Orchestral Manoeuvres in the Dark once remarked, 'we could leave the synth pop tunes to Depeche Mode now.'

He was talking as a member of the band who, apart from having one of the longest names in the history of music, were the first to play "synth pop tunes" (as opposed to songs) and get them in the charts.

Formed in 1978 by Andy and Paul Humphries – who had known each other through school in Liverpool and then in a number of short-lived electronic bands – OMD were originally just those two and a tape machine called Winston.

A single in the summer of 1979, "Electricity", brought them to people's attention, and soon they

A polyphonic synthesiser

WHAT A SYNTHESIZER DOES

Any sound is made up of three things: *pitch*, *loudness* and *timbre*. *Pitch* is how high or low a sound is. *Loudness* is how loud. *Timbre* is to do with the way a sound is made up: any sound is a complex mixture of a basic tone with various *harmonics* or *overtones*.

What a synthesizer does is enable the user to form just about any kind of sound he or she wants by providing controls to shape those three things.

Loudness, for example, is not as simple as turning the volume control up and down. On a piano, a note is loudest immediately after it has been struck, then gradually fades away. A synthesizer can also be made to play this way. Or if you like, the sound could be quietest when it starts and then get louder.

In addition to those three things, most synthesizers also contain what are called "performance controls".

Phil Oakey of The Human League (*below*) Depeche Mode (*below right*)

found themselves supporting Gary Numan on a British tour. They replaced Winston with a couple of real musicians, built their own studio in Liverpool, and before long had a hit with "Enola Gay".

These days, OMD are one of the most successful electronic bands in the world.

HUMAN LEAGUE

When the Human League first started back in 1977, their sole aim was to make massively successful pop singles using only synthesizers and voice. It took them four years to achieve that aim, and by the time they had the two original synthesists in the band – Ian Craig Marsh and Martyn Ware – had left to form Heaven 17.

When March and Ware were computer operators they teamed up with a hospital porter with lop-sided hair called Phil Oakey, and later with Adrian Wright who contributed a slide show to their live concerts.

That line-up lasted through three years, five singles and two albums before internal arguments split the group in half. The remaining two, Oakey and Wright, found singers Joanne Catherall and Susanne Suley at a Sheffield disco, and brought in Ian Burden and Jo Callis to play synthesizers. Recording sessions with ace producer Martin Rushent (who also works with Altered Images) resulted in one hit after another and a number one album *Dare*.

Jo Callis was formerly a guitarist with a number of bands before joining the League. He'd never played synthesizer before.

A drum machine

These allow a note to be changed while it is being played.

Most synthesizers take the form of keyboards, this being the simplest arrangement for what are basically a series of switches. But there are also guitar synthesizers which are played through a guitar, drum synthesizers which are hit with sticks, flute synthesizers, voice synthesizers... just about any kind you can think of.

They come in two main types: *monophonic*, on which only one note can be played at a time; and *polyphonic*, which can play several notes at the same time. They can also be *pre-set* or *programmable*. On the first kind, the different sounds it can make are already set in the machine. Synthesizers whose job it is to imitate other instruments are usually pre-set. *Programmable* means that a musician can select the sounds he or she wants. These days programmable

'Well,' he commented, 'it's something different I suppose.'

SOFT CELL

David Ball of Soft Cell – he's the one who stands at the back concentrating furiously on playing his instruments – bought his first synthesizer in 1978. He'd been fiddling around with all sorts of instruments before that.

'I was just interested in the possibilities of sound.'

He met singer Marc Almond when they were both at art college in Leeds. Marc wanted to do some kind of cabaret show, David wanted to play music, so they got together and after a debut on the *Some Bizarre* album (put together by a DJ called Stevo who's now their manager) had a massive hit with "Tainted Love".

David's main interest in the synthesizer is that it gives you 'so many different sounds at your fingertips. If you can imagine a sound, you can probably get it.'

On stage Soft Cell use a couple of tape machines which contain all their rhythm, drum and bass tracks. Over these, David plays the melodies while Marc sings.

Synthesizers also allow two people to make an awful lot of noise. 'Normally you'd have to get in an orchestra or something. It's the ideal instrument for a solo performer, which is what Marc and I both are.'

KRAFTWERK

When "The Model" turned up in the charts in early 1982, a lot of people who knew Kraftwerk only as a name were disappointed. 'It sounds just like everything else in the charts,' was a typical reaction. The difference was, it was already four years old.

Nothing could have made Kraftwerk's status as the grand-daddies of electronic music clearer. They began working in a converted shed behind Dusseldorf railway station in the early 1970s when no-one else was playing purely electronic music. Having nothing to copy, they invented many of the styles that all electronic groups now use. Synthesizers weren't very advanced then either, so they built their own.

Over the years, they've worked quietly by themselves thinking carefully about what they do, making only a few albums, watching the music they helped create growing all around them.

'I think it's a breakthrough for electronics,' one of their founding members, Ralf Hutter, commented on the new British electronic groups. 'Especially because England was always the guitar music and all that. That bored me. Terrible.'

Kraftwerk might have plenty of competition now, but they still take some beating.

A sequencer

synthesizers usually contain some kind of computer memory so that, once worked out, the settings will be remembered by the machine and returned to whenever the operator wishes. The same is true of a nifty gadget called a *sequencer*. This re-plays any sequence of notes that is fed into it as often or as quickly as you like and can be used to provide both melody and rhythm parts.

The range of different synthesizers and gadgets available to the musician is huge, and getting huger. It varies from the little Casiotone synthesizers that the Human League played on "Open Your Heart" that cost about £50, to the Linndrum machines costing thousands of pounds that play all the League's percussion.

And with computers being harnessed to synthesizers more and more these days, the range will carry on expanding.

POP GOES BRITAIN

Find out where your favourite stars come from by studying our pop music map of the British Isles.

The Jam
Modern Romance
Mari Wilson
Theatre Of Hate
Bow Wow Wow
Tenpole Tudor
Japan
Iron Maiden
Linx
Lee John of Imagination
Kim Wilde
Adam Ant
Buster Bloodvessel of Bad Manners
Bucks Fizz
Madness
Spandau Ballet
David Van Day of Dollar
Haircut 100
Depeche Mode
Steve Strange
Shakin' Stevens
Ashley Ingram of Imagination
The Jets
UB40
Toyah
Duran Duran
ABC
Heaven 17
LIVERPOOL
SHEFFIELD
BIRMINGHAM
COVENTRY
NORTHAMPTON
CAMBRIDGE
BASILDON
LONDON
BECKENHAM
BRIGHTON
NEWPORT
CARDIFF
DUBLIN
BLEEP! BLEEP!
BLIP! BLOP!
CIDER

THE HUMA

LEAGUE

JOANNE CATHERALL
Vocals
Birthdate: **18th September, 1962**
Height: **1.65 metres (5′ 5″)**
Hair: **brown**
Eyes: **brown**

PHILIP OAKEY
Vocals
Birthdate: **2nd October, 1955**
Height: **2.1 metres (6′ 1″)**
Hair: **dark brown**
Eyes: **brown**

IAN BURDEN
Synthesisers, bass guitar
Birthdate: **24th December, 1957**
Height: **1.8 metres (5′ 11″)**
Hair: **dark brown**
Eyes: **brown**

JO CALLIS
Synthesisers
Birthdate: **1st May, 1951**
Height: **1.70 metres (5′ 7″)**
Hair: **brown**
Eyes: **brown**

SUSANNE SULEY
Vocals
Birthdate: **22nd March, 1963**
Height: **1.63 metres (5′ 4″)**
Hair: **blonde**
Eyes: **grey-blue**

ADRIAN WRIGHT
Visuals, synthesiser
Birthdate: **30th December, 1957**
Height: **1.83 metres (6′)**
Hair: **ginger**
Eyes: **grey-blue**

ALTERNATIVE

Pop stars are pop stars. Or are they? Have you ever wondered what David Ball of Soft Cell would be doing if he wasn't playing synthesizers? Or how Buster Bloodvessel would bring home the bacon if he wasn't singing in Bad Manners?

No? Well, Look-in went to find out anyway, and here we reveal all. Some pop stars of course have had other jobs in the past...

Clare Grogan of Altered Images has also been an actress in Gregory's Girl.

If Sheena Easton hadn't been a pop star she would have liked to be a failed pop star.

David Ball of Soft Cell fancies himself as a chef.

If Sarah hadn't joined Bananarama she would have liked to be a footballer.

Gary Numan has always fancied himself as a pilot.

CAREERS

ri Wilson would like to work with children.

Apart from being a pop star, Toyah Willcox also has a thriving career as an actress.

ster Bloodvessel of Bad Manners and Errol Kennedy of gination would both like to model clothes.

Suggs and Lee from Madness were once decorators.

l Weller of The Jam says he'd like to be a private ective.

Hazel O'Connor wouldn't mind being an archaeologist.

Nick Heyward of Haircut 100 would like to be a tractor driver.

Sting of the Police used to be a teacher.

Eddie Tudorpole of Tenpole Tudor would like to live a life of wealth and leisure.

kim wilde

Real name: **Kim Smith**
Birthplace: **Chiswick, London**
Birthdate: **18th November, 1960**
Height: **1.65 metres (5′ 5″)**
Hair: **blonde(ish)**
Eyes: **blue**

In the pop world, stars come and go as time marches on and public tastes change. Some personalities have instant success while young – others have to wait years before achieving popular success. The luckiest span both categories, by maintaining long-term success by constantly changing and developing their style. Here Phil Parsons takes a look at some of these...

the old timers

CLIFF RICHARD

Top of everyone's list of success stories has to come Cliff. With his group, The Drifters, who later changed their name to The Shadows, Cliff recorded a demo record for only £6 way back in 1958! Then they released "Move It" which reached number two in the charts and the following year "Living Doll" got to number one.

In the early days Cliff had the greasy quiff and curling lip that made him Britain's answer to Elvis. He outgrew this rock 'n' roll style to make successful films like *The Young Ones* and *Summer Holiday* and had many hits with slower, more romantic songs.

By the mid-1970s it looked like Cliff's career was flagging but he revived it by recording stronger songs with top musicians and the last few years have seen him more successful than ever. His 1979 hit "We Don't Talk Anymore" was actually his biggest-selling single ever!

By constantly updating and changing his style, Cliff has kept many of his original fans who have grown up with him, and gained more new ones. So the age of his following has to be one of the widest there is – from grandchildren to grandparents!

Cliff hasn't changed much himself, though. He still looks as young as ever (well, almost) and he still feels the same way about his music as he did in the early days. 'However much I develop, I'm still very much a rock 'n' roll singer at heart,' says Cliff.

THE OLD ROCKERS

In the early 1960s a young singer called Paul Raven had a very minor hit with a song called "Tower Of Strength". For years he struggled to achieve success but it was not until 1972 that he had his first proper hit as... Gary Glitter! For three years Gary was one of the brightest pop stars in Britain with hits like "Do You Want To Touch Me!" and "I Love You Love Me Love". In 1976, however he announced his retirement from the pop world and performed a splendid series of farewell concerts.

But by the end of the year he was back performing and making records again. Somehow, though, a second phase of success has eluded him. He frequently appears on television, still releases records and his shows attract a kind of cult following. Through it all, he remains a cheerful showman with fans among many of today's most popular performers. The original Human League even had a hit with their own version of Gary's "Rock And Roll (Part Two)".

Another young hopeful in the

PAUL RAVEN: 1963

GARY GLITTER: 1973

SHANE FENTON: 19

1967

1972

1980

early 1960s was Shane Fenton who had a hit in 1961 with "I'm A Moody Guy". His next hit came eleven years later when he changed his name to Alvin Stardust and whizzed up the charts with a song called "My Coo-Ca-Choo". His sound brought the spirit of 1950s' rock 'n' roll up to date and gave him several more hit records. In 1979 he reappeared in the television show *Oh Boy!* alongside another early-60s' rocker, Joe Brown, and Shakin' Stevens. And in 1981 he returned to the charts with a disc that brought rock 'n' roll into the 1980s: "Pretend". Once a rocker always a rocker!

VIN STARDUST: 1982

PAUL McCARTNEY

There's nothing to be said about Paul McCartney that hasn't already been said. His career in the public eye has now spanned twenty years, from the release of The Beatles first single, "Love Me Do", in 1962, to the release of this year's hit LP, *Tug Of War*. If you followed the picture-strip story of The Beatles in *Look-in*, you'll know the story of his rise to fame. After The Beatles split, Paul embarked on a new career, partly solo, sometimes with his wife Linda, and also with his band, Wings.

Paul is so successful because he writes good songs, He also changes with the times while retaining an instantly recognisable McCartney sound. It may be a fast song like "Coming Up" or a slow, melodic tune like "Ebony And Ivory", but it will always be popular.

Apart from musical talent, Paul belongs to that generation of stars like Cliff Richard who emerged in the early 1960s. He still looks young, maybe not as youthful as the mop top who sang with The Beatles, but you've got to admit, he's well preserved!

DAVID BOWIE

As unpredictable as he is original, David Bowie is now an established figure in British music. He could be called the chameleon of pop, but that would be unfair. Bowie doesn't change his appearance to suit his surroundings, it's more like his surroundings have to change to suit him!

After several unsuccessful years of songwriting and performing, he launched into the charts in 1969 with "Space Oddity", a song inspired by the film, *2001*. Then in 1972 his career really took off again when he created the character "Ziggy Stardust". He had outrageous spikey orange hair, and wore make-up and outlandish clothes. Nothing had ever been seen like it before but it was quickly accepted and copied.

Bowie has stayed at the top because of his original ideas and his ability to change quickly. No doubt he could have kept Ziggy Stardust going for a few years but instead he quickly became "Aladdin Sane" and then took up with the "Diamond Dogs". Suddenly in 1974 he came under the spell of soul music and his style of music and dress completely changed. Crisp dance music and smart suits replaced the outrageous stance. In 1977 he changed his style yet again, experimenting with a more electronic sound, helping in the process to create a whole new style of music to which people like Gary Numan, Japan and Ultravox owe much.

In the late 1970s and early 1980s,

Bowie took up acting, starring in the films, *The Man Who Fell To Earth* and *Just A Gigolo*, in the television play *Baal*, and also in the Broadway stage play, *The Elephant Man*. Musically he's also progressed and came a full circle with the hit "Ashes To Ashes" in which Major Tom (of "Space Oddity") makes his re-entry. What next for Bowie? He'll always be busy, unpredictable and worth watching!

ABBA

Towards the end of 1973 a Swedish group called ABBA released a single in this country called "Ring Ring". It did nothing in the charts, which is hardly surprising since no one had heard of them. The following year they wowed us all with "Waterloo" at the Eurovision Song Contest and ABBA the super-group was born.

Their two-boy, two-girl line-up has frequently been copied since then, take for instance our own Euro-winners Bucks Fizz who even bleached their hair to match! In other words, ABBA were and still are trendsetters.

Unlike a lot of bands, ABBA haven't spent months and months "on the road" touring. Instead they've stayed at home and developed that distinctive sound; you always know it's an ABBA record the second you hear it!

Although their sound is instantly recognisable it doesn't mean all the records are the same. ABBA records vary so much they appeal to all ages. Their hits vary from "Eurodisco" sounds like "Lay All Your Love On Me" to haunting ballads like "One Of Us".

They have had their personal problems – Bjorn and Agnetha, and Frida and Benny's marriages have split up. But with seven number one albums and nine number one singles behind them, who's to stop Sweden's second biggest export?

STATUS QUO

Generally solo artists are around

BRYAN FERRY: 1973

BRYAN FERRY: 1981

STATUS QUO: 1968

STATUS QUO: 1982

CLIFF RICHARD: 1961

CLIFF RICHARD: 1981

for longer than groups, but one group that's an exception is Status Quo. Their publicity says they've been together for 20 years but that's a bit of a cheat really. True, the two founding members, Francis Rossi and Alan Lancaster, did get together in 1962, but to be 'Peckham's answer to jazzman Kenny Ball' – a far cry from today's hard rock!

Between then and 1967 they were in a band called The Spectres which went through several changes of line-up until they finally struck on the name Status Quo.

Their first hit was in January 1968 with the psychadelic "Pictures of Matchstick Men". They were very much a pop group then, wearing the fashionable frilly shirts of the time. However they failed to get more hits and soon hit hard times. So they began to play that familiar rock, and took to wearing jeans and T-shirts as it was all they could afford!

But over the years they built up a loyal following of "headbangers" and, even though many of their records sound all the same to some people, they've had at least one hit single every year for the past ten years – and that's something few others can boast!

ELTON JOHN

One of the best things Reginald Dwight ever did was to change his name to Elton John. Somehow his real name didn't suit the glam rock style of the early 1970s when he first became a star. At that time his outrageous specs were as well known as his big hits like "Crocodile Rock" and "Rocket Man".

By the mid-1970s Elton's style of music and dress had mellowed. But that didn't stop him being voted Worst Dressed Man in America in 1976! And it didn't stop him getting his first number one in this country with Kiki Dee for "Don't Go Breaking My Heart". The same year he announced that he intended to dedicate a lot of his time to being the Chairman of Watford Football Club.

In 1977 came what must have been the highpoint of his career – singing "Don't Go Breaking My Heart" with Miss Piggy on *The Muppet Show*. Despite the fact that everything must seem a bit of an anti-climax after that, Elton still produces very successful albums as well as undertaking mammoth world tours. As proof of his long-standing success, his most recent album *Jump Up* is his 23rd LP release!

ROXY MUSIC

Roxy were the original glam rock band formed way back in 1971. Proof that they have been around for a long time is the current revival of glam rock by bands like Duran Duran and Japan.

The key to their success also lies in change. Bryan Ferry brought new sophistication to pop, he was wearing a tuxedo when other groups were in scruffy old jeans and T-shirts. But for a while in 1977 and 1978 it seemed that the band had split up as there were no new albums, only solo releases.

However they did get back together again in 1979 once all the punk uproar had died down, and released their *Manifesto* album which produced three hit singles. But it was another year before the *Flesh And Blood* album followed it up and this year has seen the release of *Avalon*. Perhaps that's why they're still so successful, it's always something of an event when a record of theirs comes out because it's been so long since the last one!

We asked some top stars who'd made it more recently than our 'old timers' why they thought these artists and groups have been around for so long.

Peter Powell

Top Radio One DJ Peter Powell has a high opinion of Cliff. 'He is part of our musical heritage. Solo artists are in a completely different field to groups. Bands are much more trendy and popular for a while – you have people like The Human League and Adam and The Ants – but people like Cliff, and Elton John, have a much more loyal following,' says Peter.

Altered Images

When we told Clare Grogan and Johnny McElhone of Altered Images who our old timers were, they were impressed by the people on the list. Said Clare: 'I can understand why they are all in the position or league they are. Like with ABBA, they've all been fairly consistent with their songs and the quality of their songs.'

Johnny said: 'ABBA I love! They're one of my favourite bands. They're the ultimate pop band. Lately they haven't been so good, but they've been so consistent over the years. And their records are not just trash pop songs, they're classy songs.'

Just like ABBA, Johnny hopes that Altered Images will be around for a good few years. 'Our single "See Those Eyes" is more sophisticated than previous singles. We're hoping to appeal to all sorts of markets, not just one.

Adam Ant

We asked Adam what he thought of Paul McCartney because it's widely known he's one of Paul's biggest fans. 'I think Paul McCartney is the best bass player in the world. I had the first three solo McCartney albums and learned every single bass line off them!'

Phil Oakey

It may come as a surprise but the ultra-modern and fashionable Human League really admire ABBA. 'I've often said I want The Human League to be the electronic ABBA,' admitted Phil Oakey. 'They make great singles because they encompass all the best qualities a pop record should have – tune, lyrics, arrangements and production.'

Pop

So you think you know a
about pop music, huh? We
maybe you do and mayb
you don't, but here's yo

1 Before he joined The Human League, what was Philip Oakey's job? Was he (a) a gravedigger, (b) a hairdresser, (c) a hospital porter, or (d) a computer programmer?

2 The drummer who Ringo replaced in The Beatles was called (a) Stu Sutcliffe, (b) Pete Best, (c) Rory Storm, or (d) Charlie Watts?

3 Kim Wilde's real name is (a) Kate Wilde, (b) Kim Smith, (c) Kim Carnes, or (d) Marti Wilde?

4 What was the name of the film in which Clare from Altered Images appeared? Was it (a) *Chariots of Fire,* (b) *That Sinking Feeling,* (c) *Quadrophenia,* or (d) *Gregory's Girl*?

5 David Bowie's son is called (a) Ziggy, (b) Zowie, (c) Joey, or (d) Howie?

6 Gary Numan has crashed his plane (a) once, (b) twice, (c) three times, or (d) four times?

7 Which of these pop stars has got a pierced nose? (a) Frank Sinatra, (b) Dave Gahan of Depeche Mode, (c) Philip Oakey of the Human League, (d) Nick Heyward of Haircut 100.

8 In which year was Sting of The Police born: (a) 1945, (b) 1951, (c) 1955, or (d) 1962?

9 Toyah's first album was called (a) *Toyah,* (b) *Sheep Farming in Barnet,* (c) *The Corn Is Green,* or (d) *The Divine Miss Willcox*?

10 Where was Annabella of BowWowWow when she was discovered by manager Malcolm McLaren: (a) at a disco, (b) in church, (d) in hospital, or (d) in a launderette?

11 The name Duran Duran comes from: (a) a character in the film *Barbarella;* (b) a cocktail made out of brandy and fresh whipped cream; (c) an ancient Chinese philosopher; (d) nowhere in

particular?

12 ABC used to be called (a) Able Baker and the Charlies, (b) Vice Versa, (c) 123, or (d) Funk-aholic?

13 Buster Bloodvessel of Bad Manners lives (a) with his mum in Stoke Newington, London, (b) with his aunt in Reading, (c) with his grandmother in Basildon, or (d) with his two dogs and a budgie in Chelsea?

14 The lead singer of Tenpole Tudor's real name is (a) Eddie Ten-pole, (b) Eddie Tudorpole, (c) Ten-pole Tudor, or (d) Bob Kingston?

15 Which of the following has not been a single by Shakin' Stevens? (a) "The Green Door"; (b) "This Ole House"; (c) "Runaway Boys"; (d) "You Drive Me Crazy".

hance to find out. Some of
ese questions are easy,
ome of them are stinkers.
l we can say is: good luck!

16 Was Adam Ant's first album called (a) *Dick Wears White Shoes,* (b) *Dirk Wears White Sox,* (c) *Derek Wears White Sometimes,* (d) *Dan Wears White Shirts*?

17 Orchestral Manoeuvres in the Dark used to have a tape machine which they called (a) Echo, (b) Chamberlain, (c) Joe, or (d) Winston?

18 Which two members of Japan are brothers? (a) David Sylvian and Mick Karn? (b) Richard Barbieri and Steve Jansen? (c) Steve Jansen and David Sylvian? (d) Mick Karn and Richard Barbieri?

19 Hazel O'Connor was born in (a) Dublin, (b) Manchester, (c) Coventry, or (d) Istanbul?

20 Cliff Richard's real name is (a) Stuart Godard, (b) Cliff Richard, (c) Harry Webb, or (d) Gordon Sumner?

ANSWERS

1. (c)	5. (b)	9. (b)	13. (a)	17. (d)
2. (b)	6. (a)	10. (d)	14. (d)	18. (c)
3. (b)	7. (b)	11. (a)	15. (c)	19. (c)
4. (d)	8. (b)	12. (b)	16. (b)	20. (c)

GRAHAM JONES
Guitar
Birthdate: **8th July, 1961**
Birthplace: **Bridlington, Yorkshire**
Height: **1.78 metres (5′ 10″)**
Weight: **57 kgs (126 lbs)**
Hair: **blond**
Eyes: **hazel**

PHIL SMITH
Saxophone
Birthdate: **1st May, 1959**
Birthplace: **Redbridge, Essex**
Height: **1.85 metres (6′ 1″)**
Weight: **70 kgs (154 lbs)**
Hair: **ginger**
Eyes: **blue**

NICK HEYWARD
Guitar and vocals
Birthdate: **20th May, 1961**
Birthplace: **Beckenham, Kent**
Height: **1.78 metres (5′ 10″)**
Weight: **57 kgs (126 lbs)**
Hair: **fair**
Eyes: **blue**

ILFORD FOX
Congas and percussion
Birthdate: **13th February, 1958**
Birthplace: **Recklinghausen, West Germany**
Height: **1.85 metres (6′ 1″)**
Hair: **dark**
Eyes: **blue**

BLAIR CUNNINGHAM
Drums
Birthdate: **11th October, 1956**
Birthplace: **Memphis, Tennessee, USA**
Height: **1.60 metres (5′ 3″)**
Weight: **52 kgs (114 lbs)**
Hair: **black**
Eyes: **brown**

LESLIE NEMES
Bass guitar
Birthdate: **5th December, 1960**
Birthplace: **Surrey**
Height: **1.78 metres (5′ 10″)**
Weight: **57 kgs (126 lbs) approx.**
Hair: **brown**
Eyes: **green**

HAIRCUT 100

POP ON TV

Pop music shows have been on TV for over 25 years and *Neil Tennant* has sat through quite a lot of them. Tune in right now to a square-eyed view . . .

Right from the start, pop seemed natural for television. It had excitement, glamour, and an endless supply of entertainers. It was in 1956, soon after the first pop explosion, that the first real pop show in Britain hit the airwaves.

The show was called *6.5 Special* and it ran on the BBC for nearly two years. The title was suggested by the fact that it was broadcast at five past six in the evenings. The producer, Jack Good, who was to become a legendary figure in pop television, gradually developed an exciting show in which pop stars, like Tommy Steele and Terry Dene, rocked (in a quiet sort of way compared to some of today's stars) in front of a young teenage audience.

ITV's answer to *6.5 Special* was *Cool for Cats* in which young fans danced to the latest pop discs. In 1958, however, ITV lured Jack Good away from the BBC to produce *Oh Boy!* This was a real rock 'n' roll show with famous British *and* American stars featured every week. People like Cliff Richard, Marty Wilde (Kim's dad) and Billy Fury. The Americans included Gene Vincent and Eddie Cochran. The show was very popular – ask any grown-ups if they remember it – and, inspired another *Oh Boy!* series on ITV a couple of years ago.

The next notable pop shows were at the beginning of the 1960s and made early Saturday evening a glued-in-front-of-the-telly time for all pop fans. There was *Juke Box Jury* on BBC TV where famous pop and showbusiness personalities commented on the week's latest single releases. A memorable week was when all four Beatles made up the whole of the panel. If

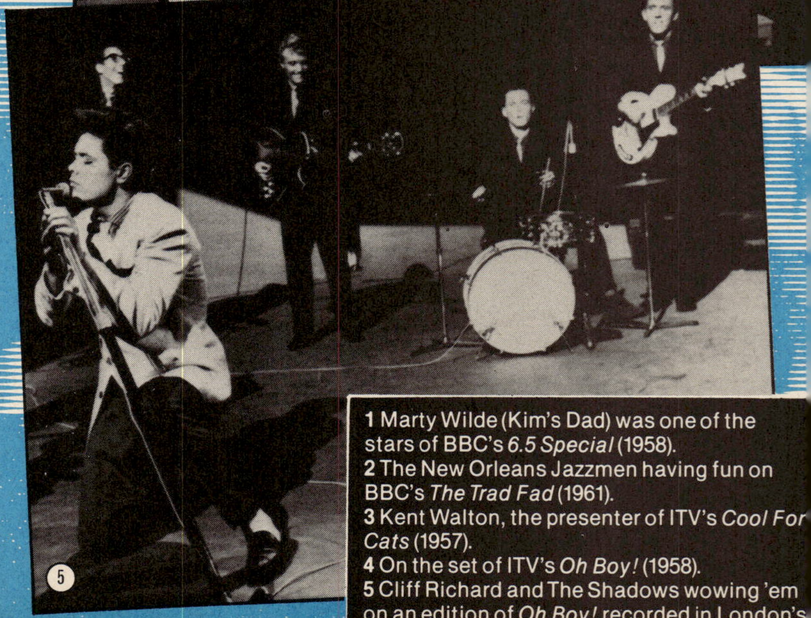

1 Marty Wilde (Kim's Dad) was one of the stars of BBC's *6.5 Special* (1958).
2 The New Orleans Jazzmen having fun on BBC's *The Trad Fad* (1961).
3 Kent Walton, the presenter of ITV's *Cool For Cats* (1957).
4 On the set of ITV's *Oh Boy!* (1958).
5 Cliff Richard and The Shadows wowing 'em on an edition of *Oh Boy!* recorded in London's Hackney Empire Theatre (1958).

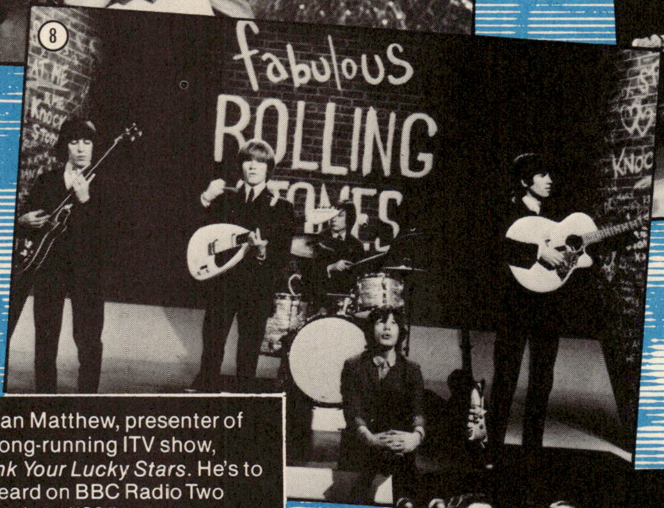

Brian Matthew, presenter of he long-running ITV show, *hank Your Lucky Stars*. He's to e heard on BBC Radio Two hese days (1961).
A bunch of pop talent on *hank Your Lucky Stars*. From eft ro right: Billy J. Kramer And he Dakotas; The Beatles; Cilla lack; The Searchers (1963).
The Rolling Stones perform on *ucky Stars – Summer Spin* 1963).

9 Part of the audience of BBC's *Juke Box Jury* help the panel to decide that a record is a hit (1961).
10 David Jacobs, used to be the chairman of *Juke Box Jury*. Now he chairs *Any Questions?* on BBC Radio Four (1961).
11 The Beatles being filmed for *The Mersey Sound*, a BBC documentary about the beat boom in Liverpool in the early Nineteen-Sixties (1963).

you switched over you could catch *Thank Your Lucky Stars* on ITV and see your fave groups and singers miming to their latest hits.

THE WEEKEND STARTS HERE!

In 1963 ITV began to broadcast the show many consider the best British pop TV show of all time: *Ready Steady Go!* It went out on Fridays at 6.30 pm, announcing that "the weekend starts here!" In the three years it lasted just about all the great acts of the time appeared, like The Beatles and The Rolling Stones. A genuinely exciting atmosphere was captured in the studio with the trendy young audience dancing and cheering. Cathy McGowan, one of the show's presenters, became a famous personality in her own right.

On New Year's Day 1964, the BBC launched a show which has become a pop institution, the programme everyone loves and hates: *Top Of The Pops*. Still going 18 years later, the formula is more or less the same now as it was all those years ago. Jimmy Saville was one of the presenters then and he still appears now. Other presenters over the years have included David Jacobs, Pete Murray, Alan Freeman, Emperor Rosko, Ed Stewart, Stuart Henry, Tony Blackburn, David Hamilton, Noel Edmonds, Dave Lee Travis, Paul Burnett, Kenny Everett, Mike Reid, Peter Powell, Simon Bates and David 'Kid' Jensen – in other words, the top BBC disc jockeys. Two DJs got their *own* television shows in the late 1960s: Alan Freeman appeared in *All Systems Freeman* on BBC and Tony Blackburn in *Time for Blackburn* on ITV.

12 The Who appearing on *Ready, Steady, Go!* (1966).
13 Studio dancers dig the music on ITV's *On The Air* (1965).
14 Cathy McGowan, the trendy presenter of ITV's *Ready, Steady, Go!* (1965).
15 Jimmy Saville introducing the first edition of BBC's *Top Of The Pops* (1964).

16 Simon Dee, the host of *Dee Time* on BBC, which featured many of the top pop stars of the time both playing and talking (1967).
17 Paul McCartney and John Lennon starred in an ITV special, *The Lennon And McCartney Show* (1965).

18 On the set of BBC's *A Whole Scene Going* (1966).
19 The Beatles rehearsing for *The Morecambe And Wise Show* (1965).
20 Peter Tork, Mickey Dolenz, Davy Jones and Mike Nesmith, collectively known as... *The Monkees* (1967).
21 Disc jockey Alan Freeman had his own show on BBC for a while, *All Systems Freeman!* Here he chats to Peter Noone of Herman's Hermits.
22 The Bay City Rollers were a pop sensation in the mid-1970s and hosted their own ITV show, *Shang-A-Lang* (1975).

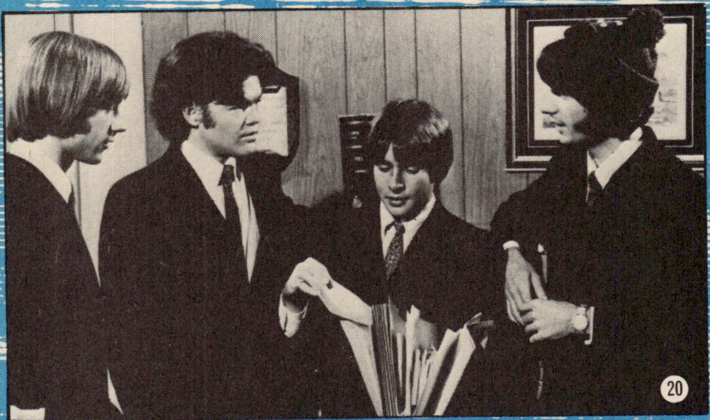

Another DJ to become a television presenter in the 1960s was Simon Dee. His chat show, *Dee Time*, was very popular for the last three years of the decade and always featured a high quota of pop stars, both singing and talking. For a while, Saturday evening was once more an essential viewing time for pop fans. *Dee Time* was shown then and was followed by... *The Monkees*!

The Monkees was an American series which began on the BBC in December, 1966. It was a nutty series centred on the kooky lives of four members of a pop group. The group themselves soon became an international pop sensation in real life with numerous hit records, like "I'm A Believer" and "Daydream Believer". The series ran until 1968 by which time its popularity and that of the group was petering out. However, old *Monkees* programmes are occasionally shown on TV today and the group still have their fans among today's pop stars–Haircut 100 for instance.

THE 1970s

As you can see, the 1960s was a good decade for pop on TV. The same cannot be said about the 1970s. For the first five years of the decade the only regular pop show on ITV was *Lift Off*, a rather dull effort, although some of the top pop names of the time, like Slade, regularly appeared on it. The BBC launched *The Old Grey Whistle Test* in 1971 aimed at late-night older rock fans. It is still going today with bands performing 'live' in the studio, film clips, album tracks and rock news. It was pretty boring when it started in 1971 and that hasn't changed much either

In 1972 another American series was first transmitted in Britain, *The Partridge Family*. It was about a family who form their own pop group (including their mother!) and make a success of it. David Cassidy, who played the eldest son, certainly made a personal success of it and became a hugely popular idol all over the world. Both The Partridge Family and David Cassidy had hit records, "I Think I Love You", for instance, and "Could it be Forever?". It didn't last forever but the rather corny television series was transmitted on and off until 1978.

Sally James acquired her first Saturday morning slot on television when in 1973 she began to host *Saturday Scene* on ITV in London. She linked together separate programmes like *Supersonic* and *Planet of the Apes* with pop records and interviews (yes, those almost legendary Sally James pop interviews!). *Saturday Scene* became so popular that it toured as a roadshow for a while and had its own British Pop Awards ceremony in 1975.

In 1974 a big, flashy pop show was launched on ITV: *Supersonic*. This show was full of stars and special effects and was unique in that its presenter was also its producer, Mike Mansfield, now famous for the videos he has made for Adam Ant. At the beginning of each show you saw him in his control box, facing a bank of monitors, wishing everyone good luck. Mike Mansfield really knew how to get the best out of the stars on his show. Gary Glitter would appear stomping about on a fire-breathing dragon being lowered down from the studio's ceiling while the Bay City Rollers would have foam jetted at them until they were completely submerged. The Bay City Rollers, who were a massive pop sensation in the mid-1970s, had their own pop show for a while called – after one of their hit songs – *Shangalang*.

Towards the end of the 1970s some quite experimental pop shows began to appear on TV. *So It Goes* attempted to liven up the normal pop show format by including funny clips from old TV programmes and some cutting comments. *Revolver* was presented by comedian Peter Cook and reflected to some extent the punk movement, with bands like The Stranglers and Siouxsie and the Banshees guesting. *The Kenny Everett Video Show* was probably the first pop show aimed at grown-ups, presumably the 1950s and 1960s pop fans who had by then grown up. Kenny Everett's zany humour dominated the show and pop stars guesting were subjected to all sorts of indignities. Of these three shows, only Kenny Everett's was really successful.

Recently, pop on TV is mainly represented by good old *Top Of The Pops*, *Razzmatazz* and *Get It Together*, while *The Old Grey Whistle Test* still plods along, greyer than ever. On reflection, much of pop on TV has been something of a disappointment over the years, probably because the powers-that-be in television are often not very interested in what's happening in the pop world, and anyway find it difficult to get a genuinely exciting atmosphere going in a television studio. However, it *has* provided some great moments and some real entertainment and the fantastic videos now being made to promote singles are constantly brightening up our television screens. Stay tuned!

23

23 Meat Loaf on BBC's *Old Grey Whistle Test* (1978).
24 David Cassidy, teen idol of the early 1970s and star of *The Partridge Family* (1973).
25 Alvin Stardust and lots of smoke on ITV's *Supersonic* (1975).
26 Mike Mansfield, the producer-presenter of *Supersonic* (1975).

24

25

26

7 Slade on ITV's *Lift Off!* (1974).
8 David Bowie was Marc Bolan's
ast guest on his series, *Marc.*
hortly after this show Marc was
agically killed (1977).
9 Gary Giltter being presented
ith the "Best Male Artist" award
y Dame Vera Lynn on the *Saturday*
cene Pop Awards. That's Sally
ames on the left (1975).
0 Bing Crosby and David Bowie
erformed an unusual duet on *Bing*
rosby's Merrie Olde Christmas
977).

31 Noel Edmonds, Maggie Philbin and Keith Chegwin, the presenters of BBC's *Multi-Coloured Swap Shop* formed a group called Brown Sauce and even had a hit record with "I Want To Be A Winner" (1981).
32 Cliff Richard with the crazy host of ITV's *The Kenny Everett Video Show* (1981).
33 Two typical teams with Mike Read on BBC's *Pop Quiz* (1981).
34 Soft Cell performing "Bedsitter" on *Top Of The Pops* (1981).

ELVIS
THE STORY
IN THE FIVE YEARS SINCE HIS DEATH, THE MUSIC OF ELVIS PRESLEY HAS CONTINUED TO THRILL AND ENTERTAIN. HERE WE WE PRESENT, REPRINTED FROM LOOK-IN, THE STOR OF HIS RISE TO FAME AND THE MOST EXCITING PHASE OF HIS CAREER WHICH ENDE WHEN HE JOINED THE ARMY...
ELVIS, KING
LE ROI EST MORT
ELVIS GESTORVEN
SOME YEARS LATER, THERE HAD BEEN ONE PARTICULAR RECORDING SESSION WHERE ELVIS HAD INSISTED ON RE-TAKE AFTER RE-TAKE, UNTIL HIS COLLEAGUES' PATIENCE HAD WO THIN...
LOOK, ELVIS. WHY WORK SO HARD? IT SOUNDS FINE TO ME!
WELL, LONG AFTER I'M GONE, WHAT I DID TODAY WILL BE HEARD BY MY FANS. I JUST WANT THEM TO GET THE BEST OF WHAT I HAD...
NOBODY CAN ARGUE WITH THAT. OKAY. LET'S TRY IT JUST ONCE MORE...
UH-HUH. OR MAYBE TWICE, OR THREE TIMES.
I'VE MADE A LOT OF MONEY, THANKS TO THOSE FANS. I'D NEVER WANT TO LET THEM DOWN.
YOU UNDERSTAND – IT AIN'T HARD FOR ME TO REMEMBER MYSELF AS A NOTHIN'... TO REMEMBER BAD DAYS...
BAD DAYS THAT STARTED IN A HOME-MADE SHANTY IN MISSISSIPPI, U.S. TOWN OF TUPELO. POPULATION 11,000. DAYS THAT BEGAN ON JANUARY 8th 1935, WHEN TWINS WERE BORN TO VERNON AND GLADYS PRESLEY...
I'M SORRY I COULDN'T SAVE THEM BOTH, SON...
I KNOW YOU TRIED, DOC. WE DO HAVE A FINE BOY...
THE TWIN, JESSE GARON, HAD DIED. YOUNG ELVIS GREW UP IN ABJECT POVERTY, BUT THE FAMILY LOOKED CALM ENOUGH WHEN ELVIS HAD REACHED TWO YEARS OLD...
A LABOURER WITH NO TRADE, VERNON PRESLEY DROVE TRUCKS FROM TIME TO TIME. WHEN HE BROUGHT THEM HOME, ELVIS WOULD PLAY IN THEIR CABS BY THE HOUR...
WHEN YOU GONNA TEACH ME TO DRIVE THIS, DADDY?
YOU DON'T NEED NO TEACHING, SON. YOU'VE BEEN ABLE TO HANDLE OUR OL' CAR SINCE YOU BEEN NINE.
THE BOY, EVEN THEN, HAD IT IN MIND TO BE A TRUCKER LIKE HIS PA. HE COULD NEVER HAVE DREAMED WHAT FATE WOULD DO TO HIM IN JUST A DOZEN SHORT YEARS...

COME ON OUTTA THERE, ELVIS. I GOTTA GO TO WORK.
AWW, JUST A FEW MINUTES MORE, DADDY. I LIKE TO PLAY!
MORE YOU PLAY, THE LESS I MAKE OUT — OR DO I HAVE TO GET YOUR MAMA TO WHUP YOU..?
OKAY, I'LL COME.
IT WAS ABOUT THAT TIME THAT THE FINAL PHASE OF WORLD WAR TWO WAS BROUGHT TO A CLOSE WHEN AMERICAN B29 BOMBERS DELIVERED THEIR FEARSOME ATOMIC PAYLOADS ON JAPAN...
NOT THAT WORLD EVENTS MADE MUCH IMPACT ON TUPELO. YOUNG ELVIS'S ONLY EXCITEMENT CAME FROM WEEKLY ATTENDANCES AT RELIGIOUS CAMP MEETINGS AND REVIVALS...
AIN'T GONNA STUDY WAR NO MORE
NO MORE NO MORE
THE BOY LIKED THE WAY THE PREACHERS JUMPED AROUND — ROUSING THEIR FLOCK. HE LEARNED TO IMITATE THEM, AND PICKED UP THE BASICS OF HARMONY IN THE SINGING...
Arthur Ranson
BUT THE WAR'S END BROUGHT MORE AND MORE COMPETITION FOR WORK AS SERVICEMEN RETURNED HOME, AND IN ELVIS'S LATER WORDS: "WE WERE BROKE, MAN. BROKE".
EITHER WE STAY HERE IN TUPELO AND STARVE OR MOVE TO MEMPHIS, TENNESSEE.
HOW CAN YOU BE SURE THINGS'LL BE ANY BETTER, VERN?
VERNON WASN'T SURE. BUT THE FAMILY LEFT ANYWAY, ALL THEIR POSSESSIONS ABOARD THEIR BEAT-UP PACKARD...
WHAT'S MEMPHIS LIKE, DADDY?
YOU'LL FIND OUT SOON ENOUGH, SON. MEBBE THE BOTH OF US CAN FIND A JOB THERE...
NONE OF THEM KNEW IT, BUT MEMPHIS WAS TO CHANGE THEIR LIVES FOR EVER. HIS BIRTHDAY CAME UP, AND ELVIS HAD WANTED A BIKE. HE DIDN'T GET IT, THOUGH. THEY GAVE HIM A GUITAR, INSTEAD...
GREAT! I — UH — I RECKON I'M GONNA PICK ME OUT A TUNE ON THIS IF IT'S THE LAST THING I DO!
THAT'S IT, SON. YOU MAKE US SOME MUSIC. IT'LL AT LEAST KEEP US CHEERFUL...

ELVIS WAS A FAST LEARNER. THE FIRST HESITATING TUNE HE MANAGED TO PICK OUT HAD A RATHER APPROPRIATE TITLE...
GONNA GET ME THE HANG OF THIS IF IT TAKES ALL WEEK!
UH—YOU MAY FIND IT TAKES A LITTLE LONGER THAN THAT, BOY...
WON'T—YOU PLAY—A SIMPLE MEL-ODY...
NOT THAT HE HAD MUCH TIME FOR PRACTICE. MORE OFTEN THAN NOT, THE GUITAR MADE A TRIP TO THE LOCAL PAWNSHOP TO RAISE A LITTLE MONEY...
THERE YOU GO. THREE DOLLARS. DON'T YOU EVER GET TIRED OF HOCKIN' THIS THING, KID?
IT'S KIND OF NECESSARY, SIR.
IT WAS 1950. AMERICA AND HER ALLIES WERE FIGHTING A NEW WAR IN KOREA. ELVIS AND HIS FAMILY WERE STILL FIGHTING THEIR OWN WAR AGAINST THE BREADLINE...
ONE WAY
MERRY CHRISTMAS
YOU GOIN' TO THE GOODFELLOWS' CHRISTMAS PARTY..?
WHAT ELSE, MAN? IT'S A FREE MEAL FOR US POOR GUYS AIN'T IT?
HE'D MAKE THE ODD TEN DOLLARS FOR SELLING HIS BLOOD TO THE BAPTIST HOSPITAL...
YOU COME HERE A LOT. WHAT DO YOU DO, FOR WORK?
I MOW A FEW LAWNS. I'M HOPING FOR A JOB AS A THEATRE USHER...
BUT FINALLY ELVIS FOUND HIMSELF DRIVING A TRUCK. HIS ORIGINAL AMBITION. IT PAID THIRTY-FIVE BUCKS A WEEK—A PRINCELY SUM TO HIM...
DRIVE IN
EAT SHOP
PEPSI
CAFE
EAT
THERE WAS A RECORD SHOP IN MEMPHIS WHERE ANYONE—FOR A SMALL FEE—COULD CUT A PRIVATE DISC. IT WAS RUN BY A MAN NAME OF SAM PHILLIPS...
IT'S MAMA'S BIRTHDAY NEXT WEEK. I'M GONNA MAKE HER SOMETHIN' SPECIAL...
SUN RECORDS
SAM PHILLIPS
OPEN
WELL, HERE GOES. I SURE HOPE THE GUYS IN HERE DON'T LAUGH AT MY VOICE OR MY PLAYIN'...
TO A YOUTH BROUGHT UP IN POVER EVEN A LITTLE MONEY MEANT A LOT. JUST FOUR DOLLARS WERE THAT YOUNG ELVIS PRESLEY COU AFFORD TO MAKE THE PRIVATE RECORD.
Arthur Ranson

HOW COULD HE HAVE KNOWN THAT WHAT HE WAS ABOUT TO DO WOULD SET HIM ON THE FIRST RUNG OF THE LADDER TO FAME ... WOULD LAY THE FOUNDATIONS OF AN ENTIRELY NEW SOUND AND LOOK FOR A GENERATION OF YOUNG PEOPLE...
... MY HAPPINESS ...
THE STUDIO WAS OWNED BY SUN RECORDS, IN MEMPHIS. THEY MADE A CRUST OUT OF HOPEFULS JUST LIKE THE SHY TRUCK-DRIVER...
ER—JUST A MINUTE.
HEY, I'M SORRY. AM I TAKING TOO MUCH TIME? I KNOW THERE ARE OTHER GUYS WANTING TO RECORD... ...
IT ISN'T THAT. I LIKE YOUR SOUND. I WANT TO DUPLICATE THIS ON TAPE, SO'S I CAN LET MR PHILLIPS HEAR IT, LATER.
OH. UH—SURE SURE... THANK YOU, MA'AM.
ELVIS REMEMBERED HAVING BEEN PUZZLED. NOT THAT IT WAS THE FIRST TIME HIS VOICE HAD BEEN ADMIRED. HE'D BEEN ENCORED AT A SCHOOL SHOW...
THEY— THEY LIKE ME..?
YOU DREW THEM LIKE A MAGNET! GO ON— SING SOME MORE!
THEY'VE GOT TO BE KIDDING! DON'T YOU KNOW WHAT THEY SAY TO ME IN CLASS?
DON'T YOU KNOW HOW THEY GET AT ME..?
ELVIS PRESLEY'S TEACHER HAD LITTLE IDEA OF THE TRUTH. OF HOW UNHAPPY HE WAS...
YAHHH! GET HIM! CUT HIS HAIR!
WHY YOU WEAR CRAZY CLOTHES LIKE THAT, PRESLEY?
HERE WERE TIMES WHEN HE REACTED...
NEVER SAW A COAT LIKE THAT ON A HUMAN BEFORE!
WHY, YOU...
NAHHHH!
BUT NOW, IT SEEMED, THINGS HAD CHANGED NOT LONG AFTER THE NINETEEN YEAR OLD HAD LEFT SUN STUDIOS...
THIS AIN'T BAD! WHAT DID YOU SAY HIS NAME WAS?
PRESLEY, ELVIS PRESLEY WHY DON'T WE PUSH THE DISC OUT LOCALLY, AS A COMMERCIAL PROPOSITION..?
Arthur Ranson

1954. THE END OF A WHOLE ERA OF POP MUSIC. 'SOFT' SINGERS LIKE DORIS DAY AND DEAN MARTIN WERE TOPPING THE CHARTS...
Arthur Ranson
ROCK AND ROLL? PHONEY AND FALSE. PLAYED FOR THE MOST PART BY CRETINOUS GOONS!
...AND FRANK SINATRA WAS CHARACTERISTICALLY OUTSPOKEN ABOUT A RAW NEW MUSIC THAT SEEMED TO MANY TO BE AN ABSURD AND TEMPORARY CRAZE...
HOW WRONG HE WAS! IN TIME, SINATRA WAS DESTINED TO ENGAGE ELVIS FOR A SPECIAL SHOW AT AN ASTRONOMICAL $150.000 FOR A SIX MINUTE APPEARANCE!
THAT HOWEVER WAS IN THE FUTURE. AT HOME IN MEMPHIS, ELVIS TOOK A PHONE CALL FROM SAM PHILLIPS, BOSS OF SUN RECORDS...
YOU MADE A PRIVATE RECORD FOR YOUR MOM, THREE MONTHS AGO. SON, I LIKE IT. I WANT YOU TO RECORD SOMETHING ELSE...
I HUNG UP AND RAN FIFTEEN BLOCKS TO MR. PHILLIPS'S OFFICE BEFORE HE'D GOTTEN OFF THE LINE!
MUCH LATER, AT THE HEIGHT OF HIS FAME, ELVIS WAS FOND OF RECALLING HIS REACTION TO THAT CALL...
PHILLIPS HAD A GOOD TRACK RECORD FOR HUNCHES. HE'D GIVEN COUNTRY AND WESTERN SINGER JOHNNY CASH AND ROCKER JERRY LEE LEWIS WHO BECAME BIG STARS THEIR FIRST BREAKS...
I WANT YOU TO CUT "BLUE MOON OF KENTUCKY", AND "THAT'S ALL RIGHT, MAMA". THAT'S A BIG BOY CRUDUP NUMBER...
YEAH, I KNOW IT.
THE DISCS WERE BIG LOCAL HITS BUT SUN RECORDS WERE HARDLY GEARED FOR NATIONWIDE DISTRIBUTION IN A COUNTRY AS HUGE AS THE USA! TWO MORE SINGLES FOLLOWED...
IT WAS WHEN A FLAMBOYANT EX-CARNIVAL PROMOTER NAMED 'COLONEL' TOM PARKER HEARD ELVIS'S MUSIC THAT THINGS BEGAN TO MOVE...
JUST LISTEN TO THIS. I'D SAY THIS BOY HAS A MILLIONS-WORTH OF TALENT!
THINKING OF TAKING A PIECE OF THE ACTION, TOM?
ALWAYS PERSUASIVE, PARKER ENGINEERED A DEAL WITH THE GIANT RECORDING COMPANY, RCA-VICTOR. AND IN 1955, THEY BOUGHT ELVIS'S CONTRACT FROM SUN FOR $35,000...
YOU AND I, BOY, ARE GOING TO CONQUER THE WORLD!

IT ISN'T ONLY THE CHINESE WHO NAME EVERY YEAR AFTER AN ANIMAL. FOR DEVOTEES OF POP MUSIC, 1956 WOULD ALWAYS BE REMEMBERED AS "THE YEAR OF THE HOUND DOG"—THANKS TO THE YOUNG MAN SIGNED UP BY RECORD COMPANY RCA-VICTOR AND BROUGHT FROM VIRTUAL OBSCURITY TO WORLD-WIDE FAME...
Arthur Ranson
ELVIS PRESLEY'S FIRST RECORD FOR HIS NEW LABEL WAS 'HEARTBREAK HOTEL'—AND SOLD A MILLION AND A HALF COPIES...
CLEAR THE WAY THERE! GANGWAY LET THE MAN THROUGH!
TAXI CAB
SINCE MUH BABY LEFT ME, AH'VE FOUND A NEW PLACE TO DWELL...
ELVIS REVELLED IN IT. HE'D JOKE WITH HIS FANS...
RIGHT FROM THE START, HIS HIP-TWITCHING, MAGNETIC STYLE HAD HIS AUDIENCES SCREAMING FOR MORE. THERE HAD BEEN NOTHING LIKE IT BEFORE. NOTHING.
THANK YOU, THANK YOU! YOU BRING A LUMP TO MY WALLET!
THE HYSTERIA GREW. GIRLS WOULD RUB THEIR HANDS ON THE STAGE WHEN HE'D LEFT—THEN KISS THEM CLEAN...
BUT EVERY STAR ALWAYS HAS CRITICS—AND IN ELVIS'S CASE, THEY WERE EVEN MORE HYSTERICAL THAN THE FANS!
HE IS A DEVIL INCARNATE! HE BRINGS OUR WORLD TO RUIN IN A WELTER OF JELLY-FISH MORALITY!
SAVE OUR CHILDREN FROM THIS FIEND, PASTOR!
ELVIS ALWAYS WORRIED ABOUT THAT SORT OF REACTION. ONCE, HE WAS ASKED IF HE THOUGHT HE SET A BAD EXAMPLE...
IF I THOUGHT THAT WAS TRUE, SIR I WOULD QUIT AND GO BACK TO DRIVING A TRUCK...
CTV
2
THERE WERE EVEN SOME TEENAGE OPPONENTS TO CONTEND WITH. ELVIS WAS DISTRESSED TO READ OF A HAPPENING IN CHICAGO...
FIVE YOUNG GUYS HANGED AN EFFIGY OF ME FROM A LAMP-POST, COLONEL TOM...
SON—AS YOU BECOME A BIGGER AND BIGGER STAR, THERE'S GONNA BE WORSE. MUCH WORSE...

BY THE AUTUMN OF 1956, ELVIS PRESLEY HYSTERIA HAD GRIPPED THE WHOLE OF THE UNITED STATES. EVERY RECORD HE MADE WAS AN INSTANT HIT, AND HIS PERSONAL APPEARANCES WERE SOLD OUT WITHIN HOURS OF ANNOUNCEMENT. A CHICAGO RADIO STATION PLAYED ELVIS DISCS NON-STOP FOR TWELVE HOURS, PROVOKING EXTRAORDINARY LISTENER-REACTIONS...
WHEN ARE YOU TAKING THE NEXT BREAK FOR NEWS..? I WANT TO HANG OUT MY WASHING BUT I DON'T WANT TO MISS A SINGLE MOMENT OF ELVIS!
THE AMERICAN ELECTIONS WERE ON. EISENHOWER WAS ABOUT T BE VOTED IN FOR ANOTHER TERM AS PRESIDENT. BUT IN LOWNDES COUNTY, MISSISSIPPI...
HEY, FELLAS. WE'VE GOT A VOTE FOR **ELVIS** AS PRESIDENT!
ABROAD, ELVIS WAS NEWS, TOO. EVEN IN LONDON, WHERE THE BRITISH-FRENCH ATTACK ON THE SUEZ CANAL IN THE MIDDLE EAST WAS MAKING PEOPLE JITTERY...
WOULDN'T BE SURPRISED IF THAT PRIME MINISTER OF OURS, EDEN, GETS US INTO A THIRD WORLD WAR.
IF **THAT** WASN'T ENOUGH, HAVE YOU HEARD THAT CHAP ELVIS PRESLEY ON THE RADIO? ABSOLUTE RUBBISH. AND MY DAUGHTER ACTUALLY **LIKES** IT!
Arthur Ranson
ELVIS WENT ON FROM STRENGTH TO STRENGTH. HIS MANAGER, 'COLONEL' TOM PARKER, WAS WORKING ALL OUT ON HIS BEHALF...
WHEE-EWWW! HOLLYWOOD **ALREADY?**
YEP, YOU'RE GONNA MAKE A FILM. IT'S ALL SIGNED AND SEALED. IT'LL BE CALLED "**LOVE ME TENDER**"...
HELD OVE FOR ANOT WEEK
IN THE SPACE OF A FEW MONTHS, THE EX-TRUCKER FROM TUPELO HAD BECOME THE CENTRE OF A TWENTY MILLION DOLLAR A YEAR INDUSTRY. A TEENAGER COULD DRESS FROM TOP TO TOE IN ELVIS GEAR...
Elvis
HIS STYLE WAS COPIE SLAVISHLY. AT BENSO HIGH SCHOOL, THE PRINCIPAL ORDERED 1,700 MALE STUDENTS GET RID OF THEIR DUC TAIL AND SIDEBURN HAIRCUTS – OR BE EXPELLED.
YOU HAVE THREE WEEKS TO RETURN TO **NORMALITY!**
FAME CARRIED ITS PROBLEMS...
MY WIFE CARRIES A PHOTO OF YOU IN HER BAG, AND SHE **DOESN'T** HAVE ONE OF ME! STEP OUTSIDE!
AW, MAN! DON'T BLAME **ME...**
ELVIS **HAD** TO DEFEND HIMSELF..
I WISH THEY WOULDN'T **DO** THAT KINDA THING... IT MAKES ME FEEL GUILTY...

NE YEAR OF SUDDEN AME HAD BROUGHT LVIS PRESLEY A LONG VAY FROM DRIVING A RUCK FOR PEANUTS E, PERSONALLY, WAS ECKONED TO BE MAKING AROUND A MILLION DOLLARS A EAR, AND WAS ORMALLY TO BE OUND AT THE WHEEL F ONE OF HIS MOUSINES...
PASSENGER CARS 10AM - 3PM MON THRU FRI
WALK
COME ON LIGHTS. CHANGE!
WHY THE HURRY? BECAUSE EVERY STOP, NO MATTER HOW SHORT, BROUGHT ITS PROBLEMS!
MADE IT!
ELL-VIS!
EEEE!
STOP!
AT ONE SHOW, FANS LOCATED HIS CAR, AND VIRTUALLY WRECKED IT IN THE PARKING LOT...
AWW, NO. WHAT A MESS!
THAT'S FAME, ELVIS. BUY ANOTHER TOMORROW.
I love You
RECORDS CONTINUED TO POUR OUT. THE FILM "JAILHOUSE ROCK" PACKED THE CINEMAS...
MUCH LATER, ELVIS RECALLED A TROUBLESOME INCIDENT OF THE TIME. IT HAPPENED IN MEMPHIS...
A MARINE CORPS PRIVATE WALKED UP TO ME, AND SAID I'D BUMPED INTO HIS WIFE A COUPLE OF MONTHS PREVIOUSLY!
WELL, I HAD A TOY GUN IN MY POCKET!
IT HAD BEEN NOTHING MORE THAN A FAKE PISTOL USED AS A FILM PROP...
OPTICIANS
BACK OFF, BUDDY!
UHH... UHHH...
Arthur Ranson
THE MARINE TOOK ELVIS TO COURT FOR THREATENING HIM WITH A 'DEADLY WEAPON'. BUT THE CASE WAS THROWN OUT...
I GUESS I WAS WARY ABOUT GUYS IN UNIFORM AFTER THAT. BUT THE FUNNY THING—WELL, YOU ALL REMEMBER WHAT HAPPENED A FEW MONTHS AFTER.
YEAH! YOU MADE THE NATION'S TEENAGERS BURST INTO TEARS!
THEN IN MARCH, 1958, ELVIS WAS CALLED UP FOR MILITARY SERVICE IN THE UNITED STATES ARMY...
UH—IT'S DOWN TO EVERY MAN TO DO HIS BIT, COLONEL TOM...
AND THE FIRST PHASE OF HIS CAREER WAS WELL AND TRULY OVER!

GET SMART

Pop fashions are pretty colourful nowadays and here's your chance to make them even more colourful. On these pages are four pop fashion styles: punk, disco, nightlife and sporty. The only trouble is, they're not in colour – not yet, that is. We've left it up to you to decide on the best colours for each outfit and then to colour them in. So get smart and start colouring!

PUNK

DISCO

N I G H T L I F E

S P O R T Y

A treat for the ears? Or a load of old rubbish?

Angus Allan turns the spotlight on...

the EUROVISION song contest

Pearl Carr and Teddy Johnson were Great Britain's first Eurovision winners in 1959 with "Sing Little Birdie".

It's been called an excruciating experience. A wretched farce. Worse than a visit to the dentist. The comments of people interviewed in the street range from shrugging acceptance, through indifference, to downright hostility. And yet around six hundred million viewers every year sit glued to their tellies when The Eurovision Song Contest hits the screen.

Why do they do it? Just for a cheap laugh when poor old Norway collects a dismal zero from the judges? To marvel at the astounding lyrics of some of the entries? True, the 1973 Swiss offering did have a line that translates into 'Tomorrow there'll be time enough to think about life, to have children, and invest all my savings. Hurray!'

No – in truth the contest does have glamour and spectacle, and that final totting-up of points can certainly induce nail-biting tension when, for example, Great Britain and their traditional rivals France are running neck and neck. Let's not be too beastly about it, the Eurovision circus has on occasion thrown up worthy numbers. Cliff Richard's "Congratulations", for a start. Though it didn't win. Then there was Sandie Shaw's "Puppet On A String", Dana's "All Kinds Of Everything", and ABBA's "Waterloo", all of which indeed bested the opposition. ABBA's winner, what's more, took a group virtually unknown outside Sweden to the pinnacle of international stardom. Lasting international stardom.

Established names, though, have occasionally come a cropper in the contest. Would you believe that Elton John actually failed the preliminary heats in 1969? Gary Glitter flunked it in 1975, too – but that was really by his own choice. He didn't like the song he was given to sing.

The Eurovision Song Contest began in 1956, when the television companies then participating in the Eurovision link decided to set it up. The first venue was Lugano, Switzerland, and appropriately

In 1962 Ronnie Carroll sang for Great Britain in Luxembourg. He looked very smart but "Ring-a-ding", the song he sang, only came fourth.

Sandie Shaw was another British winner in 1967 with "Puppet On A String".

enough, the Swiss won it with a song called "Refrains".

Great Britain entered for the first time in 1957, but our entry, "All", sung by Patricia Bredin, came nowhere. We came second in 1959 with "Sing Little Birdie" by Pearl Carr and Teddy Johnson, but we had to wait until 1967 before we actually won. That was Sandie Shaw's year of triumph.

One of the big features of the contests seems to have been the amount of squabbling involved. In 1970, leading British songwriters threatened to boycott the whole shebang when some American compositions were considered for the preliminaries. Quite rightly, they argued that a British entry should be British throughout. Then there was the hoo-hah surrounding the Irish entry in 1973, when two separately-sponsored girl singers, Maxi and Tina respectively, both considered themselves to be that country's official entry. Both flew out to Luxembourg, but it was Maxi who appeared. Her song, which contained the less-than-memorable lines 'Are the mountains blue and hazy, or am I a little crazy?', pancaked.

More seriously, politics have reared their ugly head on more than one occasion. In 1978, Jordan decided to telecast the show, but blacked out the Israeli entry from start the finish, and the following year, Turkey withdrew because the finals were to be held in Jerusalem.

Over the years, the titles of some of the entries have been a justifiable target for the critics' scorn. Among the more laughable were "Boum Ba Da Boum" (Monaco, 1967), "Oi Oi Oi" (Norway, 1969), "Pump Pump" (Finland, 1976) and "Boom Bang-a Bang" (Great Britain, 1969). The last named, however, was a joint winner for Lulu, and another champ in the same mould was Holland's "Ding Ding-a-Dong" in 1975. Never mind the titles, wince at some more lyrics. How could *anyone* enter a popular song about a hydro-electric plant surrounded by

Cliff Richard has twice represented Great Britain in the Eurovision Song Contest: in 1968 and 1973. On the first try he came second with "Congratulations".

Lulu looking excited as she arrives for the 1969 contest in Amsterdam. She was joint winner with a song called "Boom-Bang-A-Bang".

reindeer? Norway did, in 1980, thus capping the absurdity of their 1973 opus, which contained the rhyme 'Come and join us! In the game of girl and boyness!'

Are most of them, even the favourites, such forgettable songs? Well, the answer has to be yes. Whoever can remember "Ring-a-Ding Girl", which Ronnie Carroll sang for us in 1962? Or "Looking High-High-High", performed by Bryan Johnson in 1960. Even in recent years, such things as Israel's 1978 and 1979 winners, "A-Ba-Na-Bi" and "Halleluiah" are now quite beyond recall. "Making Your Mind Up" so triumphantly sung by our own Buck's Fizz last year, comes easily enough to the lips. But for how long?

The Eurovision Song Contest, traditionally hosted by the previous year's winners, costs a great deal to set up. So much so that some countries – Luxembourg is a prime example – dread ever having to lash out for it a second time. But what does winning the event mean to the singers and songwriters involved! In a word – money. Perhaps half a million pounds for the artistes, and corresponding royalties for the composers. There's certain to be a whole year of glamorous travel, and plenty of publicity. Johnny Logan, winner for Ireland in 1980, says he practically lived in a plane for eight months, and at one point toured eleven countries in the space of six days. Much good it did the poor chap in the long run, though. Right from the start, he was honest and wise enough to admit that he could well be a one-hit wonder – which unfortunately he was. And some winners found all the ballyhoo too much of a good thing all round. Like France's 1977 victor, Marie Myriam. The song that took her to the top – "The Bird And The Child" – became, she says, a nightmare. She ended up hating every syllable of it, having to perform it over and over and over again. 'Serves her jolly well right', many of the Contest's legion of critics would say!

In 1981 a bunch of British Eurovision winners flew to Norway for a winners' get-together. They were Lulu (right), Bucks Fizz (left) and Brotherhood of Man (in the middle).

Bucks Fizz celebrating with champagne the morning after they triumphed with "Making Your Mind Up" in 1981.

What it's like on the Continent, I have no idea, but here in Britain the majority of the press takes a delight, year after year, in sneering at The Eurovision Song Contest. They call it trivial, banal, boring – and all the other fashionable adjectives. Some of them get so worked up that one almost expects a mighty section of the entertainment columnist fraternity to parade violently down Fleet Street, burning songsheets, smashing records and frothing severely at the mouth. But make no mistake – any spectacle that attracts six hundred million viewers worldwide (and the Contest has frequently been screened in such far-apart places as Japan, Poland, Dubai and Sierra Leone) can't be all bad. It is, unquestionably, entertainment, however you look at it, and by no means the shallow, shoddy sham that some would have us believe. *I* was watching this year's final, and I'll bet you were, too.

In fact, it was quite a zappy affair, what with some imaginative and eye-catching routines, not the least of which was our own "One Step Further," by Bardo. They possibly deserved more points than they got, as did Portugal's entry. Portugal kicked off the contest with an appearance in "Three Musketeers" gear – even their conductor wore a broad-brimmed, feathered hat. A pity their tune was called "Bim-Bom." It might have won – ten years ago! Yet the whole thing was fun, with a big hand of applause coming for Norway, who managed to bag a few votes, and a perfectly absurd bit of nonsense from Finland, who chose to enter a pop song about a Neutron Bomb. The singer, Kojo, didn't seem in the least put out when his prancing, red-suited rendering drew a big fat zero from the judges! But one thing about it all, at least, was certain. Germany's number – "*Ein Bisschen Frieden*" – sung by Nicole, was far and away the best of the bunch, and well earned the stack of votes that made it the winner.

The only thing is – by the time you're reading this – can you actually *remember* it ...?

Nicole, the German winner of the Eurovision Song Contest in 1982, sings "Ein Bisschen Frieden" ("A Little Peace").

JAY ASTON
Birthdate: **4th May, 1961**
Birthplace: **London**
Height: **1.63 metres (5′ 4″)**
Weight: **49 kgs (105 lbs)**
Hair: **blonde**
Eyes: **brown**

BOBBY G
Birthdate: **23rd August, 1953**
Birthplace: **Epsom, Surrey**
Height: **1.71 metres (5′ 7½″)**
Weight: **61 kgs (133 lbs)**
Hair: **blond**
Eyes: **blue**

CHERYL BAKER
Birthdate: **8th March, 1955**
Birthplace: **London**
Height: **1.61 metres (5′ 3½″)**
Weight: **52 kgs (116 lbs)**
Hair: **blonde**
Eyes: **grey**

MICHAEL NOLAN
Birthdate: **7th December, 1954**
Birthplace: **Dublin**
Height: **1.70 metres (5′ 7″)**
Weight: **57 kgs (126 lbs)**
Hair: **blond**
Eyes: **blue**

HOME IS...

For the last 20 years of his life, Elvis Presley lived in a Memphis mansion called Gracelands. After he'd moved there, they named the street outside after him: Elvis Presley Boulevard.

Gracelands, which Elvis bought in 1957 for $1,000,000, had 23 rooms. Elvis painted it in gold and blue which glowed at night.

There aren't many stars who have the street they lived in named after them. Quite a few have equally lavish residences though. John Lennon, for example, owned no less than seven of the flats in the luxury apartment block he lived in in New York. He would apparently be seen by the other residents, wandering from one to another.

Elton John, always a bit of a show-off, bought his own country mansion for £380,000. Built by Henry VIII for one of his mistresses, the house stands in its own 37 acres of land and has six bedrooms, its own cinema, squash courts, a heated pool and a vast conservatory with banana and orange trees. In the grounds there are three lakes, woods and paddocks.

Chas Smash of Madness relaxes with a book in his terraced house in North London. (*Above*) Suggs of Madness at his mews house in Camden Town, London. (*Below*)

Coming down to earth a bit, Adam Ant lives in a two-room flat near Regents Park in London. He hired two young designers from the Royal College of Art to do the place up for him, and they kitted it out with marble-topped tables, blue satin chairs, and silvery green walls with matching velvet curtains.

He seems to have spent nearly as much time putting his flat together as he does putting his make-up on!

Nearby, Eddie Tudorpole of Tenpole Tudor lives in much less luxurious surroundings: a squat overlooking Regents Park that he reckons he'll get chucked out of soon.

Pop stars don't earn nearly as much money as you might imagine, especially not at first. Lots of them still live with their

After a day at the recording studio or a big live concert, what kind of homes do pop stars go back to? *Dave Rimmer* has been finding out.

parents. Mari Wilson lives in a three-bedroom terrace house in Neasden with her family. Buster Bloodvessel lives in a council flat in Stoke Newington, North London, with his mum. The Jets, who are three brothers, all still live at home in Northampton.

Others do manage to afford their own flats. Hazel O'Connor has a two-room flat in North London. David Ball of Soft Cell has quite a big flat all to himself on the top floor of a house in Leeds. Apart from a living-room and bedroom, he also has a small room to work in.

Nick Heyward of Haircut 100 divides his time between living in Beckenham, and living at the Ski Club in Victoria, London, where his Dad runs the bar. Asked in an interview last year where he'd like to live, the waggish guitarist replied:

'I'd like to live in a transparent rock where no-one can see in but I can see everyone tripping up over me.'

Doesn't sound much fun, does it?

Olivia Newton-John has a large house to herself in Los Angeles. Cliff Richard has a similar kind of place in Weybridge, Surrey. The three members of Bananarama, on the other hand, share a council flat in Holborn, London.

And not everyone is even as lucky as that. When the Human League first hit the big time, Phil Oakey didn't have anywhere to live at all! He used to sleep on a couch at the group's Monumental Pictures Studio in Love Street, Sheffield. He was asked at the time whether he'd like to move down to London.

'No,' he replied. 'London is a den of vice and iniquity.'

But when they do make some money, houses are one of the first things that pop stars buy, if only because it's quite a sensible thing to do with your cash. Depeche Mode were quite happy with living at home with their families in Basildon, but their accountant told them: buy property. One thing's for sure: if they *do* buy houses, they won't have private lakes and cinemas and they won't glow in the dark. But then, you never know . . .

Fancy living in Depeche Mode Gardens, Basildon?

Adam Ant in his flat near Regents Park in London. (*Above*)
Sting has a hideaway home near the sea on the west coast of Ireland. (*Below*)

CHARTBEAT

– THE POP GAME

TRY TO GET YOUR BAND INTO THE TOP TEN BY AVOIDING ALL THE HAZARDS ALONG THE WAY

To Play

You need a counter for each player and one dice. The game is best with three or more players. Each player chooses a counter to represent his or her pop band (use the name of your favourite band or make up a name of your own) and places it on "Start".

The players throw the dice in turn and the player who scores highest starts first. The player on the left of the starter begins next and so on. Each player throws the dice and moves clockwise that number of places, following the instructions on the shape he or she lands on. If you throw a "six" you get another throw.

The bands keep moving round and round the outer ring until they land on "Record Deal". Then, on their next turn, they start moving round and round the inner ring. The first player to throw the dice and get a score which lands him or her exactly on "Chart Action" moves into the "Top Ten" and is the winner.

The others can keep on playing if they want to for second and third place. You may find that sometimes none of the bands wins – but that's show-biz!

HOW A RECORD BECOMES A HIT

When a record enters the top twenty, it's the result of a lot of hard work by many people. *Phil Parsons* examined this hit-making process by following the progress of one of Altered Images' hit singles, "See Those Eyes", from the song being written to the single entering the charts. Here's his report.

2 RECORDING THE SINGLE

Altered Image's first album, *Happy Birthday,* was quite well received but Epic records decided their new signing needed a hit single. So they turned to producer Martin Rushent. He'd turned The Human League around and helped to make them a top pop group after years of getting nowhere in the charts. Martin did the trick with "Happy Birthday", "I Could Be Happy" and the much more sophisticated "See Those Eyes". But before the producer and the band start recording, the record company has to agree to the choice of material and how it should sound.

Annie Rosebury of Epic's A&R (artists and repertoire) department takes up the story: 'Before the actual single is recorded, the band have to record a demo tape. Then we choose which track will be the single and choose the producer. He decides what he wants to do, then we all get together and decide what to finally do.

'"See Those Eyes" was a joint decision. Altered Images have so many tracks which could be singles, but we thought this was more sophisticated. Some of the other tracks are a bit similar to the first two singles, but we can always go back to that style if we want.

Martin Rush

The first stage in having a hit is the idea for the song. Altered Images write almost all of their own material and "See Those Eyes" was no exception. The band all had a hand in writing the music but Clare wrote the words herself.

Clare and Johnny explained how "See Those Eyes" came into being. 'The music always comes first,' said Clare. Johnny continued: 'We get a rough idea of the music and build round it till we get a feel of the structure. Then Clare sings over it and we just build the music and vocals round it.'

'On the last album Clare wrote some of the words and we wrote the others. But it's far better if they're her own words because she sings them better and she knows what they mean. She's getting better at writing words. Before she seemed nervous but now she's improving and getting more cohesion to them.'

'They don't even know what half my words are!' exclaimed Clare. 'I like words to rhyme most. As long as they all rhyme I'm quite happy.'

Clare explained her lyrics for "See Those Eyes". 'It's about how girls can manoeuvre boys. In a lot of my songs I am making statements about how bold and naughty and horrible girls are! That's what it's really about, I think!'

Johnny chipped in: 'People can interpret it as they want. One person thinks it means one thing, and to another person it will be completely different.'

Some of Clare's lyrics have an unusual source of inspiration. 'I like writing about girls mostly – most of my songs are just about girls and what goes on in their heads. But I have a Winnie The Pooh book called *Now We are Six* which I get all my ideas from. I just read the poems and get ideas. It's a wonderful book and not childish at all.'

So much for the writing of a hit single, but next, in a roundabout sort of way, comes the recording.

nd his daughter) at Genetic Studios

'The crucial thing in the success of Altered Images is Martin Rushent. I used to work at Island Records with Martin. I played him a demo tape of Altered Images before they signed up with Epic. Martin said "fantastic, I've got to produce them".'

Of course once the band had signed up with a record company Martin was only too pleased to take over and produce them. The band are naturally very happy with him at the helm.

Johnny told us how a record reaches its polished final form: 'We just keep playing them live and improve. We add bits and change bits. If it's too long we cut it down and the best bits we expand.' Clare added: 'We start off one way and end up in a completely different way.

'Martin has the final say, that's why we use him. But we wouldn't do anything we didn't want to.' Johnny went on: 'If we don't agree we argue it out till we come to a decision. It's fairly democratic. He's got more ex-

Annie Rosebury

Altered Images performing "See Those Eyes" on *Top of the Pops*.

Martin Rushent

perience than us so we respect him and he respects us because we have written the songs. You can't make a bad song sound good, but Martin can make a good song sound great.'

Annie Rosebury continued with the record company's side of the story: 'The producer comes to us with what he has decided will be the finished mix. Sometimes the bass or vocals may not be quite right so it may need to be remixed. Then the record is actually cut and we are sent a test acetate. You can only play them about six times but they allow us to hear what it sounds like on vinyl. Sometimes it sounds different to the tape.

'The factory make a few test pressings of the single on ordinary vinyl. We play it again to make sure it's OK. It is important that there are no faults in records, and if we find any it will have to be re-cut.'

Annie summed up the work of her department: 'Our job is to see that recording goes smoothly and everything gets done. In a large company things can get confused.'

Once the disc has been made it has to be packaged. This is especially important for albums, but singles are quite often released in picture sleeves. This was the case with "See Those Eyes", and a lot of work is put into it.

Clare explained: 'Covers are mainly our idea then we tell David Band (a designer) and he works on it. We have to have a cover everyone likes. It's very important for it to sell. We like to keep them simple but striking.'

Johnny continued: 'If it's too complicated people can't focus on it when they walk into the shop. If you make it simple but striking they see it straight away. We were working out ideas for our *Pinky Blue* album, but it's the usual thing – you get ideas after the sleeve has been done.'

As Clare said, the responsibility for their eye-catching sleeves lies with David Band.

Like all the members of Altered Images, David is also from Glasgow. He has known Clare for some time and then got to know Gerry McElhone (Johnny's brother) who is their manager.

He studied textile design in Glasgow but has now moved to London to do a post graduate course in textile design at the prestigious Royal College of Art.

'Up until the "See Those Eyes" my designs had no relationship to the singles. But it was such an obvious thing to play on,' said David of the stylized face which appears on the sleeve of the single. 'The record company prefer them to be simple, not messy,' he added, confirming the need for 'striking but simple' designs.

But designing a sleeve is no easy task. 'Some of them I do in half an hour and I'll take them to CBS and they'll like them. But some take a couple of weeks and they'll reject them.

'I didn't study graphics so I don't have a clue about layout. I get into a lot of trouble from CBS for just presenting them with bits of artwork,' said David.

However we're sure you'll agree that David's design is really eye-catching and well worth the trouble he put into it.

David Band

Vince Connolly

Once you have the finished product you have to make sure that everyone knows about it. Vince Connolly of the Epic promotions department told us how he sets about this.

'We send the record round to all the radio stations two weeks before it was released to try to maximize the amount of airplay, which should hopefully create a demand for the record.

'We also send copies along to *Top of the Pops* and hope they'll pick it out if it makes it into the charts. If it enters at around 42 to 45 in the charts then there's a good chance of the group appearing on the programme. This happened with "See Those Eyes" and normally after appearing on the show they really take off.

'We also send videos to all the TV stations and usually organize posters so that you get the name of the act across so they become accepted. Altered Images have a good acceptance on TV and radio. Then we just have to hope producers like it and make sure it gets played.'

It is also important that the public gets to know all about the band. That means organizing interviews in magazines, newspapers and on TV and radio. Mike Wilkie is a press officer at Epic and Altered Images is one of the bands he looks after.

Mike Wilkie

This is how he explains his link in the chain of making a record a hit. 'We'll hear the single, and discuss how to "package" it in the media. About a month before the single is released we decide how we want the band to look and choose a photographer. I also write the biography with details of the band, the single and a tour if there is one.

'Then we usually give an exclusive interview to a publication whose readership are likely to buy the record. We sift through the people wanting to interview the band and decide who'll give the best coverage. (As usual *Look-in* was the first in line!) We give them as much time as possible.

'After that I sort through a cross-section of teenage magazines, national newspapers and music papers. It's a well planned series of events.

'Once the single has been released I begin to run the operation down and begin to think about the album or the next single and start work on publicising that . . .

'I have to reach a delicate balance between the press, radio and TV. We have to get the publicity into as many homes as possible.'

TOP 75 SINGLES

	This Week	Last Week	Wks on Chart	TITLE Artist (producer) Publisher		Label number (distributor)
	1	1	6	SEVEN TEARS Goombay Dance Band (Petersen) Southern		Epic EPC A1242 (C)
	2	4	5	JUST AN ILLUSION Imagination (Swain/Jolley) Red Bus (International)	○	R&B RBS 208 (A)
	3	3	5	QUIEREME MUCHO (YOURS) Julio Iglesias (Arcusa) Peter Maurice/EMI		CBS A1939 (C)
	4	7	5	LAYLA Derek and The Dominoes (Dominoes) Throat		RSO 87 (F)
▲	5	33	2	MY CAMERA NEVER LIES Bucks Fizz (Andy Hill) Paper Music/Big Note		RCA 202 (R)
	6	2	11	THE LION SLEEPS TONIGHT Tightfit (Friese-Greene) Cromwell Music	●	Jive JIVE 9 (C)
£	7	14	4	AIN'T NO PLEASING YOU Chas & Dave (Hodges/Peacock) Chasdave Music		Rockney KOR 14 (A)
	8	6	7	POISON ARROW A.B.C. (Trevor Horn) Copyright Control		Neutron/Phonogram NT 102 (F)
£	9	16	3	GHOSTS Japan (Nye) Chadwick Nomis/Virgin		Virgin VS 472 (C)
	10	9	7	PARTY FEARS TWO The Associates (Associates/Hedges) APB Music		Associates ASC 1 (W)
£	11	18	4	DAMNED DON'T CRY Visage (Visage/Ure) Various		Polydor POSP 390 (F)
	12	8	10	CLASSIC Adrian Gurvitz (Gurvitz) Rak		RAK 339 (E)
	13	5	9	MICKEY Toni Basil (Mathieson/Veitch) Chinnichap/Rak	●	Radialchoice/Virgin TIC 4 (C)
£	14	21	4	HAVE YOU EVER BEEN IN LOVE Leo Sayer (Mardin) Paper Music		Chrysalis CHS 2596 (F)
▲	15	35	2	GIVE ME BACK MY HEART Dollar (Trevor Horn) Perfect Songs/Island		WEA BUCK 3 (W)
£	16	23	4	IS IT A DREAM Classix Nouveaux (Solo) Chappell		Liberty BP 409 (E)
▲	17	41	2	SEE THOSE EYES Altered Images (Martin Rushent) Warner Bros		Epic EPC A2198 (C)
	18	NEW		MORE THAN THIS Roxy Music (Davies/Roxy Music) EG Music		EG/Polydor ROXY 3 (F)
£	19	22	5	YOUR HONOUR Pluto (Khouri) April Music		KR KR4 (R)
	20	11	10	GO WILD IN THE COUNTRY Bow Wow Wow (Brian Tench) Copyright Control	○	RCA 175 (R)
	21			DON'T LOVE ME TOO HARD		
	39	25	8	SOME GUYS HAVE ALL THE LUCK Robert Palmer (Palmer) Kirschner/Warner Brothers		Island WIP 6754 (E)
	40	17	8	CENTERFOLD J. Geils Band (Justman) Rondor	○	EMI America EA 135 (E)
	41	37	3	A NEW FASHION Bill Wyman (Wyman/Kysey) Rondor		A&M AMS 8209 (C)
	42	NEW		STONE COLD Rainbow (Roger Glover) Thames Talent		Polydor POSP 421 (F)
£	43	48	3	FIVE MILES OUT Mike Oldfield (Oldfield/Newman) Virgin		Virgin VS 464 (C)
£	44	43	3	EMPIRE SONG Killing Joke (Killing Joke/Plank) Energy Music		Malicious Damage/Polydor EGO 4 (F)
£	45	72	2	AMOUR AMOUR Mobiles (Lynton) Servecity (Leosong)		Rialto RIA 5 (P)
	46	31	5	BAAL'S HYMN (EP) David Bowie (Visconti/Bowie) Universal Edition		RCA BOW 11 (R)
£	47	52	2	LOVE POTION NO 9 Tygers Of Pan Tang (Peter Collins) Carlin		MCA 769 (C)
£	48	66	2	I RAN A Flock Of Seagulls (Mike Howlett) Zomba Music		Jive JIVE 14 (C)
	49	42	4	THIS BEAT IS MINE Vicky 'D' (Turner/Booth) April		Sam/Virgin VS 486 (C)
	50	NEW		PAPA'S GOT A BRAND NEW PIGBAG Pigbag (Hunt/O'Dell) Mistral/Warner Bros		Mistral Y Y10 (RT)
£	51	67	2	RUBY RED Slade (Slade) Whild John Music		RCA 191 (R)
	52	32	7	HEAD OVER HEELS Abba (Andersson/Ulvaeus) Bocu		Epic EPC A2037 (C)
	53	NEW		A CELEBRATION U2 (Steve Lillywhite) Island		Island WIP 6770 (E)
	54	39	8	TOWN CALLED MALICE/PRECIOUS The Jam (Pete Wilson & The Jam) Chappell	●	Polydor POSP 400 (F)
	55	46	3	I HATE . . . PEOPLE Anti-Nowhere League (Aurable) Head Music		WXYZ ABCD 2 (P/FP)
	56	50	3	TEMPORARY BEAUTY Graham Parker (Douglas/Parker) Street Music		RCA PARK 100 (R)
	57	NEW		EVER SO LONELY Monsoon (Jones/Coe) Indipop/Virgin Mobile Suite Corp		Phonogram COPR 2 (F)
	58	NEW		DON'T CALL IT LOVE (WILDLIFE EP) Girlschool (Nigel Gray) Acton Green		Bronze BRO 144 (F)
	59	30	6	DEUTSCHER GIRLS The Original Acam & The Ants (–) EG Music		EG/Polydor EGO 5 (F)

▲ position increase over last week, position 21-50 25% sales increase over last week

A-Z TOP WRITERS

A Bunch Of Thyme (Trad: Hurley) . . . 24
A Celebration (U2) . . . 53
Ain't No Pleasing You (Hodges/Peacock) . . . 7
Amour Amour (Madge/Blundell/Smithson/Lynton) . . . 45
A New Fashion (Wyman) . . . 41
The Antmusic EP (Ant) . . . 61
Are You Lonesome Tonight (Turk/Handman) . . . 28
Baal's Hymn (Brecht/Muldowney) . . . 46
Ball And Chain (Moulding) . . . 60
Blue Eyes (Osborne) . . . 31
Cardiac Arrest (Smash/Foreman) . . . 29
Celtic Soul Brothers (Rowland/Paterson/Billingham) . . . 63
Centerfold (Justman) . . . 40
Classic (Gurvitz) . . . 12
Damned Don't Cry (Strange/Ure/Currie/Egan/Formulla) . . . 11
Dear John (Gustafson/Macauley) . . . 25
Deutscher Girls (Ant) . . . 59
Don't Call It Love (Wildlife EP) (McAuliffe/Johnson) . . . 58
Don't Love Me Too Hard (Findon/Myers/Puzi) . . . 21
Empire Song (Killing Joke) . . . 44
Ever So Lonely (Coe) . . . 57
Five Miles Out (Oldfield) . . . 43
Ghosts (Sylvian) . . . 9
Give Me Back My Heart (Darlow/Horn) . . . 15
Go Wild In The Country (McLaren/Ashman/Gorman/Barbarosa) . . . 20
Have You Ever Been In Love (Hill/Sinfield/Danter . . . 14
Head Over Heels (Andersson/Ulvaeus) . . . 52
House On Fire (Geldof) . . . 30
I Can Make You Feel Good (Hewett/Jackson) . . . 35
I Hate . . . People (Animal/Magoo) . . . 55
I Ran (Score/Score/Maudsley/Reynolds) . . . 48
Iron Fist (Kilmister/Clarke/Taylor) . . . 33
Is It A Dream (Solo) . . . 16
I Will Love You (Paxton) . . . 73
I Won't Let You Down (Hymas/Diamond) . . . 74
Just An Illusion (Jolley/Swain/John/Ingram) . . . 2
Klactoveesedstein (Reilly/Bonsioni/Bynoe/Sullivan) . . . 66
...ordon) . . . 4
...Tonight . . . 6
...ne
...hillips) . . . 64
...World
...ies)
...eywood)
...ner

5 INTO THE CHARTS

The people who have the responsibility for seeing just how many homes Mike Wilkie and co. have got the single into lies with the British Market Research Bureau who compile the weekly charts that appear on *Top of The Pops* and on Radio One.

The work is paid for by the BBC and the record companies, and a music trade paper. The BMRB have a panel of 750 record shops all round the country. They include all sorts of record stores, from the big chains like Woolworths to small independent shops.

These 750 shops all keep a diary of the number of singles sold and this is collected every Saturday evening by the BMRB.

Pam Sellers of the BMRB explains what happens then: 'We use a third of the diaries, that is 250. It's done on a rotational basis, so no shop is certain to be used every week.

'When the diaries arrive here at 6.30 on Monday morning they are checked and a balanced sample is taken. The details are put on computer punch cards by the afternoon. The computer works all through the night then at 5.15 on Tuesday mornings we start working on the results.

'All the data is in the form of the record's serial number, so then we have to identify them. Some records have several different serial numbers because they are released as 7-inch, 12-inch or picture discs. So we have to add them all together.

'Then we usually have the charts ready by 9 o'clock for the BBC.'

And that is how a single like "See Those Eyes" becomes a chart success. Not quite as simple as it seems!

HOW SUCCESSFUL WAS IT?

"See Those Eyes" went straight into the charts at number 17, and stayed there the following week. It then moved up to number 11 for its third week on the charts. However it then began to go down, so it wasn't quite as big a hit as everyone thought it would be.

We asked bass player Tony McDaid what he thought about it. 'We were surprised. It went straight in at 17 which is really high. Then the second week it stayed at 17. It was demoralising. I can't think of another record that has gone in as high as 17 then not moved at all. You'd expect it to go up at least two or three places.

'But it *did* get to number 11 which I think is really good. I don't think it was a mistake to release a more sophisticated single. We all really liked it. It got the most critical acclaim we've had, but who wants that? We'd rather it sold more!'

Altered IMAGES

ANTHONY McDAID
Bass guitar
Birthdate: **15th November, 1962**
Birthplace: **Glasgow**
Height: **2.1 metres (6′ 1″)**
Weight: **67 kgs (147 lbs)**
Hair: **black**
Eyes: **don't know!**

JAMES McKINVEN
Guitar
Birthdate: **30th December, 1910!**
Birthplace: **Glasgow**
Height: **between 1.52 and 1.83 metres (5′ and 6′)**
Weight: **60 kgs (132 lbs)**
Hair: **brown**
Eyes: **blue**

CLARE GROGAN
Vocals
Birthdate: **17th March, 1962**
Birthplace: **Glasgow**
Height: **1.55 metres (5′ 1″)**
Weight: **between 41 and 48 kgs (91 and 105 lbs)**
Hair: **mousey**
Eyes: **blue**

MICHAEL ANDERSON
Drums
Birthdate: **4th December, 1962**
Birthplace: **Glasgow**
Height: **1.66 metres (5′6″)**
Weight: **48 kgs (105 lbs)**
Hair: **various**
Eyes: **green**

JOHN McELHONE
Guitar
Birthdate: **21st April, 1963**
Birthplace: **Glasgow**
Height: **1.83 metres (6′)**
Weight: **70 kgs (154 lbs)**
Hair: **black**
Eyes: **green**

QUOTE

Most of today's top pop stars have spoken to *Look-in* at some time or another. For this quiz we've looked through our files and chosen some

1 Here's two quotes from two members of the same group.
(A) *We don't know what it's like to have a flop. Everything we've released, the albums and the singles, have been hits.*
(B) *We can't help being compared with ABBA. All Eurovision bands get stuck with a label.*

2 This quote is a bit of a surprise!
To be honest, I was never much of an Elvis fan.

3 Who described their sound as: *A cross between ABBA and Depeche Mode?*

4 This is two girl singers describing how they joined their respective groups.
(A) *I had a part time job in a dry cleaners. One Saturday I was singing along to the radio when he came in. He asked me if I wanted to audition to sing in a group. I thought he was joking!*
(B) *He asked us to join. He'd only ever seen us dance, he'd never met us, heard us sing, or anything like that.*

5 Who described his hobby as: *Making camps up in my bedroom for friends?*

6 *We've always got to work on dance routines for each song. And they've danced their way into the top twenty many times!*

f Haircut 100. **6** The Nolans – Maureen Nolan talking. **7** Kim Wilde. **8** Buster Bloodvessel of Bad Manners.
The Jets – Ray Cotton talking. **10** Sally James talking about Cliff Richard. **11** Clare Grogan of Altered
nages appeared in *Gregory's Girl*. **12** Adam Ant.

characteristic quotes from our pop interviews. All you've got to do is work out who's doing the talking each time. Answers are at the bottom of the page.

UNQUOTE

7 She always looks great but she told *Look-in*: People don't usually recognise me at jumble sales. I usually go looking a bit scruffy.

8 I don't like pickled onions much, as some people think. My favourite food is probably my mum's beef stew. I eat about four or five pints of it at once. Name this food fan!

9 There are three brothers in this band and one of them told us about their early days. We learnt all the songs we would play from just one 50s compilation LP. And if the numbers had more than four chords we had to forget about them!

10 Who is talking about whom in this quote? He's so nice to interview. I've interviewed him five or six times and would love to again. He's one of those people who you just have to say "Hello, how are you?" and he starts talking away.

11 I'm not bothered about doing any more acting, because to me the band is more important than anything else. Name this singer, her band, and the film she appeared in.

12 My videos are like three-minute Hollywood spectaculars. And they cost as much! 'Nuff said?

1 Bucks Fizz – Mike Nolan and Cheryl Baker talking. **2** Shakin' Stevens. **3** Dollar – Thereza Bazar talking. **4** (A) Annabella Lwin talking about how Malcolm McLaren asked her to join Bow Wow Wow. (B) Susanne Sulley telling how Phil Oakey asked her and Joanne Catherall to join The Human League. **5** Nick Heywar

"It was the Eighties, there was a recession and people wanted value for money. I gave it to them. I was glamorous in a Hollywood way; my videos are like three-minute Hollywood spectaculars. And they cost as much! The public took to me because what I offered was so simple and colourful."

That's one way Adam Ant has explained his incredible success. Here we present a photographic look back at Adam's career with quotations taken from the many interviews he has given over the last couple of years.

ADAM ANT: WORDS & PICTURES

"I thought I owed it to the kids to give them something spectacular."

"Why did I choose the name Adam Ant? I've always liked the name Adam and have an adamant sort of character. And ants are always around and always working."

"It was very difficult when I first started. Everyone was laughing at me and telling me I was a joke."

"Every artist has one regret and mine is the film **Jubilee**. *What we thought was a very sincere attempt to create a fashion was presented as a freak show with Jordan and I as the oddities. If anything we were ahead of our time."*

(Adam and his co-star in *Jubilee* Jordan, in 1978

"I don't get recognized so much like this. But I still wear make-up. I've been using it for years. When I first started putting it on I used to get into a lot of trouble. Old ladies used to shout at me whenever I went to the shops."

"I was looking for an alternative to Western music, rock 'n' roll and decadence, and I found myself drawn to Red Indian music. This led to the warrior ideal. I always interpreted warriors as being violent, but I found out that they were supposed to be above violence and that they were honourable and had beauty and individuality within their tribe. I'd been reared on cowboy films and I'd always thought that Indians were savages who scalped people."

"I like a quiet life. I spend a lot of time writing letters, answering fan letters and thinking out new ideas for clothes and the band, reading or just looking at television."

"Meeting Princess Margaret meant more to me than meeting any star. I was terribly nervous. She told me that she loved the sound of our two drummers and she said that her children are fans of the band."

"I have as much respect for someone like Liberace as Bryan Ferry, because I think the two are in the same family of entertainment. It's simply showbusiness . . ."

(Marco dressed as the famous pianist and showman, Liberace, in the "Antrap" video.)

"People like Dick Turpin and pirates were outside society, folk heroes, and that appeals to me. In the seventeenth and eighteenth centuries being a pirate was the only way a common man could become a noble."

"Style is very, very time-consuming."

ADAM ANT

Real name: **Stuart Goddard**
Birthdate: **3rd March 1954**
Birthplace: **London**
Height: **1.71 metres (5′ 7½″)**
Weight: **67 kgs (147 lbs)**
Hair: **brown**
Eyes: **green-blue**

LOOK-IN

Round the table with Gar
Numan and Cheryl Bake

Elliott and Kendall

Sam

Elizabeth

Carl

POP PANEL

Now it's your turn to face the music. Pop, of course. Ten lucky *Look-in* readers saw stars recently, when we invited them along to put some pop posers to Gary Numan and Bucks Fizz's bubbly blonde singer, Cheryl Baker. Over tea and sandwiches Ben, Bonnie, Emma, Janey, Carl, Elizabeth, Elliott, Kendall, Polly and Sam had their chance to chat to Cheryl and Gary. To ask them all, what you the readers, have always wanted to know, and until now, never had the opportunity to ask. First in the firing line was Gary, with a whole host of questions to answer about his plane. Over to you kids!

Ben: When did you first get interested in planes?

Gary: I've been fascinated by flying for quite a few years now. But I got my first plane about eighteen months ago, just after I got my pilot's licence.

Sam: How many times have you crashed? (Laughter all round at this one!)

Gary: I've only actually crashed once. But it was a pretty bad one. I wrote off my plane and the four of us in it at the time were pretty lucky to escape unhurt. I think my dad was the only person to suffer injury – and he just cut his lip.

I've actually just bought what's left of the plane from the insurance company. I'm going to have the whole of the plane – it's a Cessna 210 – rebuilt and then I'm going to mount it on a pole, fit it with flashing lights and have it nose-diving towards the ground in the crash position. This "monument" is going in my back garden. And it will remind me what a lucky escape I had from near-disaster.

Elliott: What's the furthest distance you've ever flown?

Gary: Well, I've just come back from a round-the-world trip, so I guess you can't really fly much further than that!

(So, from planes to pop. First off, a few questions for Cheryl.)

Bonnie: Who writes your songs?

Cheryl: Most of our songs are written by a man called Andy Hill. He wrote "Making Your Mind Up", which was of course our first big hit. He's very nice. He's got black curly hair and he's very handsome.

Kendall: What would you be if you weren't a singer?

Cheryl: Well, before I did this full time, I was a secretary. But I've been singing ever since I was a little girl. And even when I was a secretary during the day, I was still singing with various groups in my spare time. But I think I'd like to have acted if I hadn't been a singer. Because that's still something I'd quite like to do one day.

Carl: How long does it take to rehearse and make a record?

Cheryl: Ooh that's a difficult one. It really all depends. First we have to get together, sort out who's going to be singing what and then go through the song. Once we've recorded it, we work out a dance routine to go with it. It usually takes a few weeks from start to finish. But often we're

Bonnie Ben Polly Emma and Janey

working on more than one song at once.

Emma: Who designs all your clothes?

Cheryl: Jay (Aston – Bucks Fizz other girl singer) does all the designing, and her mum and sister make them all for us. So, it's a real family affair.

Ben: Do you like football and what team do you support?

Cheryl: Well, my local team is West Ham. They're just up the road from where I live, so I suppose you could say I supported them. But I don't really ever go to the matches. I prefer watching snooker and darts on the telly.

Gary: I don't really like football. I used to go to matches. But since I've become famous it is a bit difficult. I went once, and some of the supporters hassled me. So I don't go anymore. I'll be watching the World Cup on the TV though. But I'm not a great sports fan. I don't play anything myself. I actually live on a golf course (in Wentworth, Surrey). But I don't play at all.

Polly: What are your favourites

out of your own songs?
Cheryl: Well, "Making Your Mind Up" has a special place in my heart, because it was the one that started it all for us. But my own personal favourite is "Land Of Make Believe", because it's such a lot of fun to sing.
Gary: "We Are Glass", which was quite a big hit for me, is my favourite song.
Janey: Have you ever lost your voice when you've been singing?
Cheryl: Yes, I did once lose it very badly whilst I was actually on stage. It was dreadful, because it happened in this song where I had to do all the high bits. The audience seemed to think it was pretty funny though. And in the end I started giggling too. As usual!
Polly: What music did you like when you were our age?
Cheryl: I loved The Monkees. I think their music was wonderful. And I had a terrible crush on them all, especially Davy Jones.
Gary: I liked The Monkees too. I used to wear this hat and mime to all their records when my friends came round.
Janey: Where does the name "Bucks Fizz" come from?
Cheryl: Well the lady who looks after us, our boss, Nicky, named us after her favourite drink, Bucks Fizz, which is, of course, Champagne and Orange juice.

Good thing for us, her favourite wasn't light and bitter!

Elizabeth: Do you get tired?

Cheryl: Yes I do. I love my sleep. I could sleep for days sometimes when I'm really tired. Luckily, my mum always gets me up in the morning. Or I'd probably snooze all day.

Polly: What embarrasses you most?

Cheryl: Well, not many things. But I think making mistakes on stage can be pretty embarrassing. I'm the sort of person though, that if I do the wrong step, I start giggling, and so do the audience. But I think my most embarrassing moment must have been when I once fell over!

Gary: I remember I had a really embarrassing moment once with a microphone. I did this big dramatic turn and got all caught up in the mike lead. It's very hard trying to keep a straight face when you're trying to untangle yourself.

Carl: What are your favourite pop groups at the moment?

Gary: Well I like a new young band called Huang Chung, who I think could be very big stars. I certainly hope so.

Cheryl: I love Madness. I think they're great because they play wonderful songs and they're all so...well, mad!

Emma: Have you got any hobbies?

Cheryl: Yes. I love crosswords. I do one every day. Usually, when I'm in bed, just before I go to sleep. In fact if I don't do one, I don't feel comfortable. I find it really helps me wind down after a busy day.

Gary: Well, every spare minute I have, will usually find me down at the airfield. Flying and everything connected with it is my biggest obsession I suppose.

Bonnie: Does music run in your family, and what do they think about your success?

Gary: No it certainly doesn't run in mine.

Cheryl: Nor mine either, although, as a family, we've always been very keen on music.

Gary: Of course my family are very involved in my career. My parents both help me run the whole operation, and my younger brother, John, who's now 17, is coming on tour with us as a drum roadie. He wants to be a drummer himself one day. And he's written his own songs. They're pretty good actually. But I think the fact that all my family are so involved in my music, says for itself what they think about it.

Cheryl: I don't come from a musical family at all. But ever since I can remember I've been singing, and Mum and Dad have always been ones for a singalong. They're very pleased about my success of course. Mum's very sensible about it though. Keeps a very level head about it all. My dad's dead proud of me. He's always going round telling people: 'My daughter, Cheryl is in Bucks Fizz you know.'

Elizabeth: What was the first record you ever bought?

Cheryl: Mine, I shouldn't think you've ever heard of. It's a record called "Rosie" by Don Partridge. My first LP was *Abbey Road* by The Beatles.

Gary: My first records were Monkees and T. Rex singles. But I can't remember which ones.

Kendall: What do you do in your spare time?

Cheryl: Well I certainly don't have very much of that at the moment. But what spare time I do have is all spent with my boyfriend. We go up to our house, which we've just bought, and go round and see our families. We're hoping to get married very soon, but I see so little of him at the moment, that I don't want to actually get hitched until I can see more of him all the time. When things have quietened down a bit for Bucks Fizz.

Gary: I crash planes! Seriously, I do spend a lot of time down my local airfield. Even if I'm not flying myself, I can sit there for hours just watching the planes. At the moment I'm learning how to do acrobatic stunts – it's great fun. I did a loop-the-loop the other day.

Polly: Did you have any nicknames when you were at school?

Gary: I was called Wally.

Cheryl: I don't think I'm going to tell you. Oh alright then. I got called Crudge a lot. Don't ask me why. It's a horrible nickname.

Carl: What were your best and worst subjects at school?

Cheryl: Maths was my worst subject. I was terrible at it. English was my best.

Gary: Carpentry was my worst – I was hopeless. Maths, believe it or not, I was pretty good at.

Emma: How do you decide what to sing about?

Gary: Well I read books and sometimes titles of songs are just lines from books. Also, you read

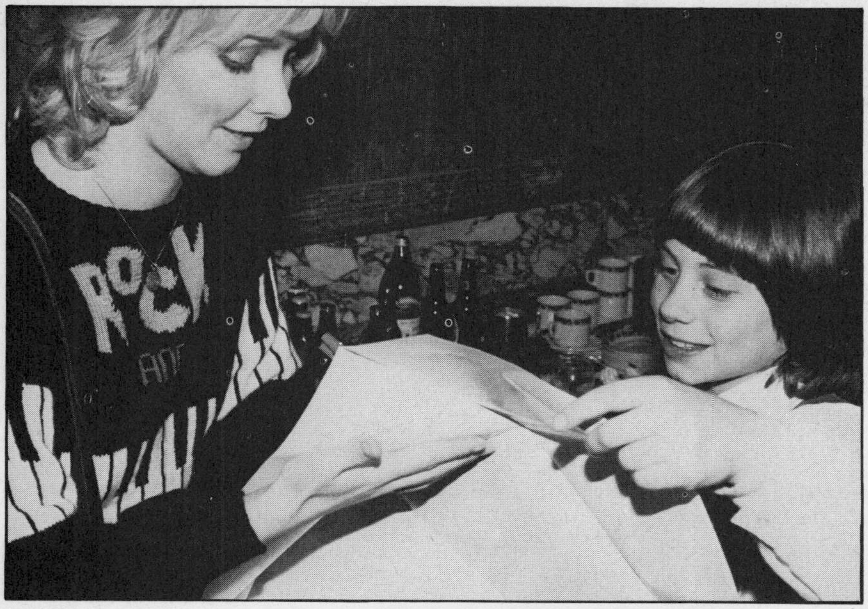

something and it gives you an idea for a song. My first hit, 'Are Friends Electric', just came to me after reading a book which put the idea in my head.
Bonnie: Did you sing as kids?
Cheryl: I used to sing all the time. Around the house, in the bath, at school, on the bus. Everywhere.
Gary: Not really. I was in the school choir though.
Elizabeth: Have you kept in touch with your schoolfriends?
Gary: No. I don't think I see anyone now from my schooldays.
Cheryl: I do. I've had the same friends since I was about 14. They've known me since before I was famous, so they don't let me get too big for my boots or put on airs and graces. They're great. I get together with them whenever I can. But that's not as often as I'd like.
Elliott: Who would you most like to meet?
Gary: Chuck Jaeger – who's a world famous test pilot.
Cheryl: I'd just love to meet Prince Charles because I think he's so cute. And of course, Princess Diana. She's lovely too.
Sam: What are your favourite films?
Gary: *The Battle of Britain*.
Cheryl: *Airplane*. I laugh all the way through it, even though I've seen it loads of times.
Polly: Do you feel famous?
Gary: Well I've been famous now for three years so I don't think about it. Of course I like doing what I'm doing. But the fame side of it I don't particularly enjoy. I like meeting fans but I hate interviews, photos etc.

Cheryl: Yes I do. And, although I love being recognised, I do sometimes wish I was leading a normal life again. Sometimes it's lovely of course. But there is the odd occasion when you just wish no-one would notice you. Not very often though. I love my work.
Sam: Do you think people are surprised at what you're like in real life?
Cheryl: No. Obviously, I don't have my stage gear on. But I look pretty much the same. A bit smaller, maybe. I think they sometimes expect me to be snooty. And I'm not, one bit.
Gary: I think people are often a bit surprised when they meet me. They always say: 'Coo, ain't he short!' And they're always saying, 'Go on Gary, give us a smile.' But I think they find me pretty friendly too.
Elliott: What's your favourite food?
Cheryl: Everything. The more fattening it is the better. I love food. Italian is a big favourite.
Gary: Chicken and chips without a doubt. I could eat it all the time.
Ben: Why do you wear make-up?
Gary: Well, it looks dramatic. And of course it does grab attention. Anyway, why not? My mum buys it for me though. Just the cheapo brands.
Cheryl: I like wearing make-up. It makes me feel glamorous. I do all my own making-up now. I know exactly the look I want.
Sam: Do you like travelling?
Gary: Yes. I love it. Particularly of course, by air.
Cheryl: No I hate it. Sometimes I wish I could just wake up in Manchester or Liverpool or wherever it is we have to go. And I hate flying. I'm terrified really. Especially at take off.

That brought our interview to an end. Gary and Cheryl then chatted away to everyone over more tea and cakes, signed photos and had their pictures taken.

As they were leaving, the last words we heard from the pop pair were Gary offering to take Cheryl up in his plane, to help her get over her fear of flying. Happy landings!